NATURAL LANGUAGE PROCESSING
WITH PYTHON AND SPACY

NATURAL LANGUAGE PROCESSING WITH PYTHON AND SPACY

A Practical Introduction

by Yuli Vasiliev

**no starch
press**

San Francisco

Publisher: William Pollock
Production Editors: Kassie Andreadis and Laurel Chun
Cover Illustration: Gina Redman
Photography: Igor Shabalin
Developmental Editor: Frances Saux
Technical Reviewers: Ivan Brigida and Geoff Bacon
Copyeditor: Anne Marie Walker
Compositor: Happenstance Type-O-Rama
Proofreader: James Fraleigh
Indexer: Beth Nauman-Montana

For information on distribution, translations, or bulk sales, please contact No Starch Press, Inc. directly:
No Starch Press, Inc.
245 8th Street, San Francisco, CA 94103
phone: 1.415.863.9900; info@nostarch.com
www.nostarch.com

A catalog record of this book is available from the Library of Congress.

About the Author

Yuli Vasiliev is a programmer, freelance writer, and consultant specializing in open source development, Oracle database technologies, and natural language processing (NLP). Currently, he works as a consultant for the bot project Porphyry. The bot implements NLP techniques to give meaningful responses to user questions. A demo can be accessed at @Porphyry_bot in Telegram.

About the Technical Reviewer

Ivan Brigida was born and raised in Krasnodar, Russia. He holds a Computer Science degree from Moscow State University and an MA in Economics from the New Economic School. He worked for several years as a financial analyst, and later moved to Google to become a digital advertising analyst. Currently, he is doing BI analytics and developing machine learning models for the Online Partnerships Group at Google, specializing in mobile app monetization.

BRIEF CONTENTS

CONTENTS IN DETAIL

INTRODUCTION

Increasingly, when you call the bank or your internet provider, you might hear something like the following on the other end of the line: "Hello, I am your digital assistant. Please ask your question." Today, robots can talk to humans using natural language, and they're getting smarter. Even so, very few people understand how these robots work or how they might use these technologies in their own projects.

Natural language processing (NLP)—a branch of artificial intelligence that helps machines understand and respond to human language—is the key technology that lies at the heart of any digital assistant product. This book arms you with the skills you need to start creating your own NLP applications. By the end of this book, you'll know how to apply NLP approaches to real-world problems, such as analyzing sentences, capturing the meaning of a text, composing original texts, and even building your own chatbot.

Using Python for Natural Language Processing

If you want to develop an NLP application, you can choose among a wide range of tools and technologies. All the examples in this book are implemented with Python code that employs the spaCy NLP library for Python. Here are some compelling reasons why you might want to choose Python and spaCy for your NLP development.

Python is a high-level programming language known for the following features:

Simplicity   If you're new to programming, Python is a good language with which to start, because it's extremely easy to learn. Due to its simplicity, Python allows you to write code that others can easily understand. For example, Python's simplicity helps chatbot developers collaborate with linguists who don't have much programming experience.

Prevalence   Python is one of the most popular languages. The vast majority of the widely used APIs have Python wrappers that you can easily install using the `pip` installation tool. The ability to install Python wrappers via the `pip` simplifies the process of obtaining third-party tools you might want to use in your NLP applications.

Significant presence in the AI ecosystem   There are a lot of Python libraries available in the AI ecosystem. This availability simplifies the development of your NLP applications, allowing you to choose among a range of libraries to best solve a particular task.

The spaCy Library

This book uses spaCy, a popular Python library that contains the linguistic data and algorithms you'll need to process natural language texts. As you'll learn in this book, spaCy is easy to use because it provides container objects that represent elements of natural language texts, such as sentences and words. These objects, in turn, have attributes that represent linguistic features, like parts of speech. At the time of this writing, spaCy offered pretrained models for English, German, Greek, Spanish, French, Italian, Lithuanian, Norwegian Bokmål, Dutch, Portuguese, and multiple languages combined. In addition, spaCy offers built-in visualizers that you can invoke programmatically to generate a graphic of the syntactic structure of a sentence or named entities in a document.

The spaCy library also natively supports advanced NLP features that other popular NLP libraries for Python don't. For example, spaCy natively supports word vectors (discussed in detail in Chapter 5), unlike the Natural Language Toolkit (NLTK). When using the latter, you would need to use a third-party tool like Gensim, a Python implementation of the word2vec algorithm.

With spaCy, you can customize existing models or individual model components, and you can train your own models from scratch to meet your application's requirements (you'll learn how to do this in Chapter 10). You can also connect the statistical models trained by other popular *machine learning (ML)* libraries, such as TensorFlow, Keras, scikit-learn, and PyTorch. In addition, spaCy can operate seamlessly with other libraries in Python's AI ecosystem, allowing you to, for example, take advantage of computer vision in your chatbot application, as you'll do in Chapter 12.

Who Should Read This Book?

This book is for those interested in learning how to use NLP in practice. In particular, it might be interesting to people who want to develop chatbots for businesses or just for fun. Regardless of your background or experience with NLP or programming, you'll be able to follow the code examples provided in this book because they all include detailed explanations of the process involved.

Some working knowledge of Python will be helpful, because the book doesn't cover the basics of Python syntax. Also, the examples assume a school-level understanding of English grammar and syntax. The Appendix is a reference for some of the less well-known linguistic concepts. If you have a good understanding of NLP concepts and some basic programming, the examples will be even easier to follow.

What's in the Book?

Natural Language Processing with Python and spaCy begins with a brief introduction to the basic elements and methods of the NLP technology used to process and analyze natural language data. Then it proceeds with increasingly complicated techniques that you can use to deal with even the sophisticated challenges that natural language can pose for computer processing and analysis. The "Try This" sections in each chapter will help you reinforce the material you just learned.

Here's what you'll find in each chapter:

Chapter 1: How Natural Language Processing Works   Provides a brief introduction to the basic elements of NLP technology. It describes the machine learning techniques that generate the data NLP libraries use, such as spaCy, including statistical language modeling and statistical neural network models used for solving NLP problems. It then describes the tasks and challenges an NLP application developer faces.

Chapter 2: The Text-Processing Pipeline   Explains what spaCy is and what it's designed to do, and then shows you how to get started with it quickly. It covers setting up your working environment and then coding using the text-processing pipeline, a series of basic NLP operations used to determine the meaning and intent of a discourse.

Chapter 3: Working with Container Objects and Customizing spaCy Covers spaCy's architecture, focusing on the central data structures available in the library. You'll get hands-on experience with spaCy's key objects by following the examples provided. You'll also learn how to customize the pipeline components to suit your application's needs.

Chapter 4: Extracting and Using Linguistic Features   Illustrates how to extract linguistic features, such as dependency labels, part-of-speech tags, and named entities. You'll learn to generate and then walk up the dependency tree of a sentence, exploring syntactic relations. By doing so, you'll learn how to programmatically continue a conversation with a chatbot user, condense long text, and complete other useful tasks.

Chapter 5: Working with Word Vectors   Explains how spaCy's models map natural language words to vectors of real numbers, allowing you to do math with words. You'll learn how to use spaCy's similarity method, which compares the word vectors of container objects to determine the closeness of their meanings.

Chapter 6: Finding Patterns and Walking Dependency Trees   Dives into the details of meaning extraction, syntactic dependency parsing, noun chunking, and entity recognition. You'll complete all the steps needed to extract meaning from raw text, using word sequence patterns and walking dependency trees. The chapter introduces spaCy's Matcher tool to find patterns and also covers when you might still need to rely on context to determine the proper processing approach.

Chapter 7: Visualizations   Discusses how to take advantage of spaCy's built-in displaCy visualizer, which you can use for visualizing syntactic dependencies and named entities in your browser. Visualizing can help you immediately identify patterns within your data.

Chapter 8: Intent Recognition   Demonstrates intent extraction, which is a common task in chatbot development. You'll learn how to extract meaning from text data, a typically challenging task that takes just a few lines of code in Python.

Chapter 9: Storing User Input in a Database   Teaches you how to automatically extract keywords from user input and store them in a relational database, which you can then use to fill out order forms or other business documents.

Chapter 10: Training Models   Covers how to train spaCy's named entity recognizer and dependency parser to meet requirements of your application not covered by spaCy's default models. It details how to train an existing, pretrained model with new examples and a blank one from scratch.

Chapter 11: Deploying Your Own Chatbot   Guides you through the process of deploying your chatbot app to Telegram, a popular messenger service, so it can interact with users over the internet.

Chapter 12: Implementing Web Data and Processing Images   Shows how your chatbot can extract answers to questions from Wikipedia and react to user-submitted images by using spaCy along with some other libraries in Python's AI ecosystem.

Appendix: Linguistic Primer   Contains a brief guide to the grammar and syntax elements discussed most frequently in the book. Readers who don't come from linguistic backgrounds can use it as a reference.

1

HOW NATURAL LANGUAGE PROCESSING WORKS

In the 19th century, explorers discovered *rongorongo*, a system of mysterious glyphs on the island of Rapa Nui (commonly known as Easter Island). Researchers have never succeeded in decoding rongorongo inscriptions or even figuring out whether those inscriptions are writing or proto-writing (pictographic symbols that convey information but are language independent). Moreover, although we know that the creators of the glyphs also erected Moai, the large statues of human figures for which the island is most famous, the builders' motivations remain unclear. We can only speculate.

If you don't understand people's writing—or the way in which they describe things—you most likely won't understand the other aspects of their life, including what they do and why they do it.

Natural language processing (NLP) is a subfield of artificial intelligence that tries to process and analyze natural language data. It includes teaching machines to interact with humans in a natural language (a language that developed naturally through use). By creating machine learning algorithms designed to work with unknown datasets much larger than those two dozen tablets found on Rapa Nui, data scientists can learn how we use language. They can also do more than simply decipher ancient inscriptions.

Today, you can use algorithms to observe languages whose semantics and grammar rules are well known (unlike the rongorongo inscriptions), and then build applications that can programmatically "understand" utterances in that language. Businesses can use these applications to relieve humans from boring, monotonous tasks. For example, an app might take food orders or answer recurring customer questions requesting technical support.

Not surprisingly, generating and understanding natural language are the most promising and yet challenging tasks involved in NLP. In this book, you'll use the Python programming language to build a natural language processor with spaCy, the leading open source Python library for natural language processing. But before you get started, this chapter outlines what goes on behind the scenes of building a natural language processor.

How Can Computers Understand Language?

If computers are just emotionless machines, how is it possible to train them to understand human language and respond properly? Well, machines can't understand natural language natively. If you want your computer to perform computational operations on language data, you need a system that can translate natural language words into numbers.

Mapping Words and Numbers with Word Embedding

Word embedding is the technique that assigns words to numbers. In word embedding, you map words to vectors of real numbers that distribute the meaning of each word between the coordinates of the corresponding word vector. Words with similar meanings should be nearby in such a vector space, allowing you to determine the meaning of a word by the company it keeps.

The following is a fragment of such an implementation:

```
the 0.0897 0.0160 -0.0571 0.0405 -0.0696  ...
and -0.0314 0.0149 -0.0205 0.0557 0.0205  ...
of -0.0063 -0.0253 -0.0338 0.0178 -0.0966 ...
to 0.0495 0.0411 0.0041 0.0309 -0.0044    ...
in -0.0234 -0.0268 -0.0838 0.0386 -0.0321 ...
```

This fragment maps the words "the," "and," "of," "to," and "in" to the coordinates that follow it. If you represented these coordinates graphically, the words that are closer in meaning would be closer in the graph as well. (But this doesn't mean that you can expect the closer-in-meaning words to be grouped together in a textual representation like the one whose fragment is shown here. The textual representation of a word vector space usually starts with the most common words, such as "the," "and," and so on. This is the way word vector space generators lay out words.)

A graphical representation of a multidimensional vector space can be implemented in the form of a 2D or a 3D projection. To prepare such a projection, you can use the first two or three principal components (or coordinates) of a vector, respectively. We'll return to this concept in Chapter 5.

Once you have a matrix that maps words to numeric vectors, you can perform arithmetic on those vectors. For example, you can determine the *semantic similarity* (synonymy) of words, sentences, and even entire documents. You might use this information to programmatically determine what a text is about, for example.

Mathematically, determining the semantic similarity between two words is reduced to calculating the cosine similarity between the corresponding vectors, or to calculating the cosine of the angle between the vectors. Although a complete explanation of calculating semantic similarity is outside the scope of this book, Chapter 5 will cover working with word vectors in more detail.

Using Machine Learning for Natural Language Processing

You can generate the numbers to put in the vectors using a machine learning algorithm. *Machine learning*, a subfield of artificial intelligence, creates computer systems that can automatically learn from data without being explicitly programmed. Machine learning algorithms can make predictions about new data, learn to recognize images and speech, classify photos and text documents, automate controls, and aid in game development.

Machine learning lets computers accomplish tasks that would be difficult, if not impossible, for them to do otherwise. If you wanted to, say, program a machine to play chess using a traditional programming approach in which you explicitly specify what the algorithm should do in every context, imagine how many if...else conditions you'd need to define. Even if you succeed, users of such an application will quickly discover weak points in your logic that they can take advantage of during the game until you make necessary corrections in the code.

In contrast, applications built on machine learning algorithms don't rely on predefined logic but use the capability to learn from past experience instead. Thus, a machine learning–based chess application looks for positions it remembers from the previous games and makes the move that leads to the best position. It stores this past experience in a statistical model, which is discussed in "What Is a Statistical Model in NLP?" on page 8.

In spaCy, aside from generating word vectors, machine learning allows you to accomplish three tasks: *syntactic dependency parsing* (determining the relationships between words in a sentence), *part-of-speech tagging* (identifying nouns, verbs, and other parts of speech), and *named entity recognition* (sorting proper nouns into categories like people, organizations, and locations). We'll discuss all of these at length in the following chapters.

The life cycle of a typical machine learning system has three steps: model training, testing, and making predictions.

Model Training

In the first stage, you train a model by feeding your algorithm a large body of data. For these algorithms to give you reliable results, you must provide a sufficiently large volume of input—significantly more than the rongorongo tablets, for instance. When it comes to NLP, platforms like Wikipedia and Google News contain enough text to feed virtually any machine learning algorithm. But if you wanted to build a model specific to your particular use case, you might make it learn, for example, from customers using your site.

Figure 1-1 provides a high-level depiction of the model training stage.

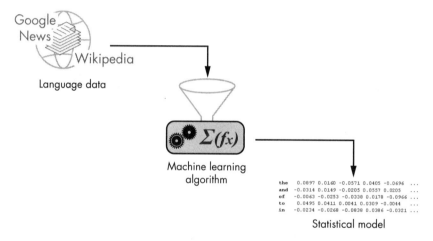

Figure 1-1: Generating a statistical model with a machine learning algorithm using a large volume of text data as input

Your model processes large volumes of text data to understand which words share characteristics; then it creates word vectors for those words that reflect those shared characteristics.

As you'll learn in "What Is a Statistical Model in NLP?" on page 8, such a word vector space is not the only component of a statistical model built for NLP. The actual structure is typically more complicated, providing a way to extract linguistic features for each word depending on the context in which it appears.

In Chapter 10, you'll learn how to train an already existing, pretrained model with new examples and a blank one from scratch.

Testing

Once you've trained the model, you can optionally test it to find out how well it will perform. To test the model, you feed it text it hasn't seen before to check whether it can successfully identify the semantic similarities and other features learned during the training.

Making Predictions

If everything works as expected, you can use the model to make predictions in your NLP application. For example, you can use it to predict a dependency tree structure over the text you input, as depicted in Figure 1-2. A *dependency tree structure* represents the relationships between the words in a sentence.

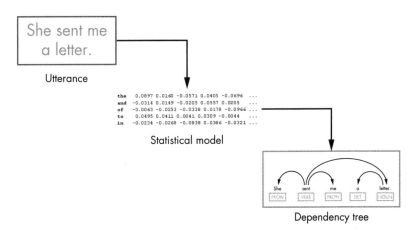

Figure 1-2: Predicting a dependency tree structure for an utterance using a statistical model

Visually, we can represent a dependency tree using arcs of different lengths to connect syntactically related pairs of words. For example, the one shown here tells us that the verb "sent" agrees with the pronoun "she."

Why Use Machine Learning for Natural Language Processing?

Your algorithm's predictions aren't statements of fact; they're typically calculated with a degree of certainty. To achieve a higher degree of accuracy, you'll need to implement more complicated algorithms, which are less efficient and less practical to implement. Usually, people strive to achieve a reasonable balance between accuracy and performance.

Because machine learning models can't predict perfectly, you might wonder whether machine learning is the best approach for building the models used in NLP applications. In other words, is there a more reliable approach based on strictly defined rules, similar to the one used by compilers and interpreters for processing programming languages? The quick answer is no. Here's why.

To begin with, a programming language contains a relatively small number of words. For example, the Java programming language consists of 61 reserved words, each of which has a predefined meaning in the language.

By contrast, the *Oxford English Dictionary,* released in 1989, contains 171,476 entries for words in current use. In 2010, a team of researchers at Harvard University and Google counted about 1,022,000 words in a body of digitized texts containing approximately 4 percent of all books ever published. The study estimated that the language would grow by several thousand words a year. Assigning each word to a corresponding number would take too long.

But even if you tried to do it, you'd find it impossible, for several reasons, to determine the number of words used in a natural language. First of all, it's unclear what really counts as an individual word. For example, should we count the verb "count" as one word, or two, or more? In one scenario, "count" might mean "to have value or importance." In a different scenario, it might mean, "to say numbers one after another." Of course, "count" can also be a noun.

Should we count inflections—plural form of nouns, verb tenses, and so on—as separate entities, too? Should we count *loanwords* (words adopted from foreign languages), scientific terms, slang, and abbreviations? Evidently, the vocabulary of a natural language is defined loosely, because it's hard to figure out which groups of words to include. In a programming language like Java, an attempt to include an unknown word in your code will force the compiler to interrupt processing with an error.

A similar situation exists for formal rules. Like its vocabulary, many formal rules of a natural language are defined loosely. Some cause controversy, like *split infinitives*, a grammatical construction in which an adverb is placed between the infinitive verb and its preposition. Here is an example:

```
spaCy allows you to programmatically extract the meaning of an utterance.
```

In this example, the adverb "programmatically" separates the preposition and infinitive "to extract." Those who believe that split infinitives are incorrect could suggest rewriting the sentence as follows:

```
spaCy allows you to extract the meaning of an utterance programmatically.
```

But regardless of how you feel about split infinitives, your NLP application should understand both sentences equally well.

In contrast, a computer program that processes code written in a programming language isn't designed to handle this kind of problem. The reason is that the formal rules for a programming language are strictly defined, leaving no possibility for discrepancy. For example, consider the following statement, written in the SQL programming language, which you might use to insert data into a database table:

```
INSERT INTO table1 VALUES(1, 'Maya', 'Silver')
```

The statement is fairly self-explanatory. Even if you don't know SQL, you can easily guess that the statement is supposed to insert three values into table 1.

Now, imagine that you change it as follows:

```
INSERT VALUES(1, 'Maya', 'Silver') INTO table1
```

From the standpoint of an English-speaking reader, the second statement should have the same meaning as the first one. After all, if you read it like an English sentence, it still makes sense. But if you try to execute it in a SQL tool, you'll end up with the error missing INTO keyword. That's because a SQL parser—like any other parser used in a programming language—relies on hardcoded rules, which means you must specify exactly what you want it to do in a way it expects. In this case, the SQL parser expects to see the keyword INTO right after the keyword INSERT without any other possible options.

Needless to say, such restrictions are impossible in a natural language. Taking all these differences into account, it's fairly obvious that it would be inefficient or even impossible to define a set of formal rules that would specify a computational model for a natural language in the way we do for programming languages.

Instead of a rule-based approach, we use an approach that is based on observations. Rather than encoding a language by assigning each word to a predetermined number, machine learning algorithms generate statistical models that detect patterns in large volumes of language data and then make predictions about the syntactic structure in new, previously unseen text data.

Figure 1-3 summarizes how language processing works for natural languages and programming languages, respectively.

A natural language processing system uses an underlying statistical model to make predictions about the meaning of input text and then generates an appropriate response. In contrast, a compiler processing programming code applies a set of strictly defined rules.

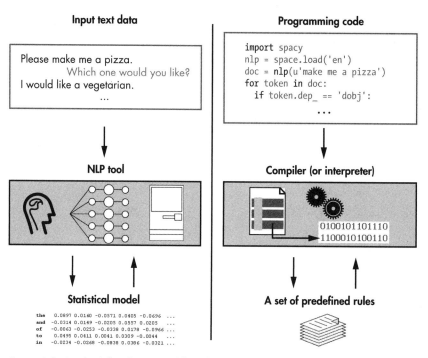

Figure 1-3: On the left, a basic workflow for processing natural language; on the right, a basic workflow for processing a programming language

What Is a Statistical Model in NLP?

In NLP, a *statistical model* contains estimates for the probability distribution of linguistic units, such as words and phrases, allowing you to assign linguistic features to them. In probability theory and statistics, a *probability distribution* for a particular variable is a table of values that maps all of the possible outcomes of that variable to their probabilities of occurrence in an experiment. Table 1-1 illustrates what a probability distribution over part-of-speech tags for the word "count" might look like for a given sentence. (Remember that an individual word might act as more than one part of speech, depending on the context in which it appears.)

Table 1-1: An Example of a Probability Distribution for a Linguistic Unit in a Context

VERB	NOUN
78%	22%

Of course, you'll get other figures for the word "count" used in another context.

Statistical language modeling is vital to many natural language processing tasks, such as natural language generating and natural language understanding. For this reason, a statistical model lies at the heart of virtually any NLP application.

Figure 1-4 provides a conceptual depiction of how an NLP application uses a statistical model.

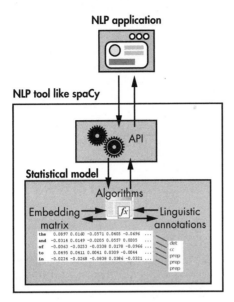

Figure 1-4: A high-level conceptual view of an NLP application's architecture

The application interacts with spaCy's API, which abstracts the underlying statistical model. The statistical model contains information like word vectors and linguistic annotations. The linguistic annotations might include features such as part-of-speech tags and syntactic annotations. The statistical model also includes a set of machine learning algorithms that can extract the necessary pieces of information from the stored data.

In real systems, a model's data is typically stored in a binary format. Binary data doesn't look friendly to humans, but it's a machine's best friend because it's easy to store and loads quickly.

Neural Network Models

The statistical models used in NLP tools like spaCy for syntactic dependency parsing, part-of-speech tagging, and named entity recognition are neural network models. A *neural network* is a set of prediction algorithms. It consists of a large number of simple processing elements, like neurons in a brain, that interact by sending and receiving signals to and from neighboring nodes.

Typically, nodes in a neural network are grouped into layers, including an input layer, an output layer, and one or more hidden layers in between. Every node in a layer (except the output layer) connects to every node in the successive layer through a connection. A connection has a weight value associated with it. During the training process, the algorithm adjusts the weights to minimize the error it makes in its predictions. This architecture enables a neural network to recognize patterns, even in complex data inputs.

Conceptually, we can represent a neural network as shown in Figure 1-5.

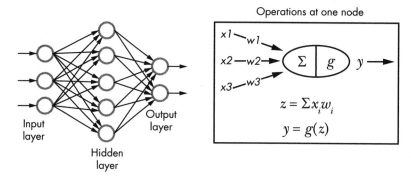

Figure 1-5: A conceptual depiction of the neural network layout and operations at one node

When a signal comes in, it's multiplied by a weight value, which is a real number. The input and weight values passed on to a neural network generally come from the word vectors generated during the network training.

The neural network adds the results of the multiplications together for each node; then it passes the sum on to an activation function. The activation function generates a result that typically ranges from 0 to 1, thus producing a new signal that is passed on to each node in the successive layer, or, in the case of the output layer, an output parameter. Usually, the output layer has as many nodes as the number of possible distinct outputs for the given algorithm. For example, a neural network implemented for a part-of-speech tagger should have as many nodes in the output layer as the number of part-of-speech tags supported by the system, as illustrated in Figure 1-6.

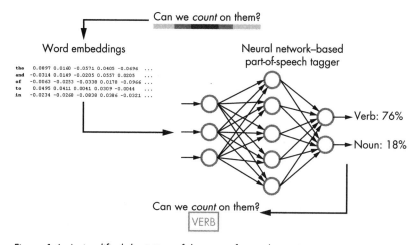

Figure 1-6: A simplified depiction of the part-of-speech tagging process

The part-of-speech tagger then outputs a probability distribution over all possible parts of speech for a given word in a given context.

Convolutional Neural Networks for NLP

The architecture of a real neural network model can be quite complex; it's formed by a number of different layers. Thus, the neural network model used in spaCy is a *convolutional neural network (CNN)* that includes a convolutional layer, which is shared between the part-of-speech tagger, dependency parser, and named entity recognizer. The convolutional layer applies a set of detection filters to regions of input data to test for the presence of specific features.

As an example, let's look at how a CNN might work for the part-of-speech tagging task when performed on the sentence in the previous example:

Can we count on them?

Instead of analyzing each word on its own, the convolutional layer first breaks the sentence into chunks. You can consider a sentence in NLP as a matrix in which each row represents a word in the form of a vector. So if each word vector had 300 dimensions and your sentence was five words long, you'd get a 5×300 matrix. The convolutional layer might use a detection filter size of three, applied to three consecutive words, thus having a tiling region size of 3×300. This should provide sufficient context for making a decision on what part-of-speech tag each word is.

The operation of a part-of-speech tagging using the convolutional approach is depicted in Figure 1-7.

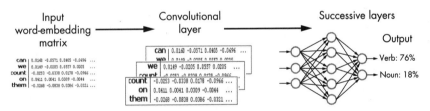

Figure 1-7: A conceptual look at how the convolutional approach works for an NLP task

In the preceding example, the most challenging task for the tagger is to determine what part-of-speech the word "count" is. The problem is that this word can be either a verb or a noun, depending on the context. But this task becomes a breeze when the tagger sees the chunk that includes the "we count on" word combination. In that context, it becomes clear that the word "count" can be only a verb.

A detailed look under the hood of the convolutional architecture is beyond the scope of this book. To learn more about the neural network model architecture behind statistical models used in spaCy, check out the "Neural Network Model Architecture" section in spaCy's API documentation.

What Is Still on You

As you learned in the preceding section, spaCy uses neural models for syntactic dependency parsing, part-of-speech tagging, and named entity recognition. Because spaCy provides these functions for you, what's left for you to do as the developer of an NLP application?

One thing spaCy can't do for you is recognize the user's intent. For example, suppose you sell clothes and your online application that takes orders has received the following request from a user:

```
I want to order a pair of jeans.
```

The application should recognize that the user intends to place an order for a pair of jeans.

If you use spaCy to perform syntactic dependency parsing for the utterance, you'll get the result shown in Figure 1-8.

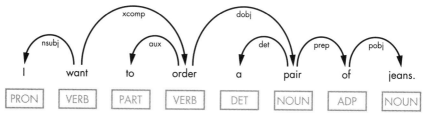

Figure 1-8: The dependency tree for the sample utterance

Notice that spaCy doesn't mark anything as the user's intent in the generated tree. In fact, it would be strange if it did so. The reason is that spaCy doesn't know how you've implemented your application's logic and what kind of intent you expect to see in particular. Which words to consider the key terms for the task of intent recognition is entirely up to you.

To extract the meaning from an utterance or a discourse, you need to understand the following key aspects: keywords, context, and meaning transition.

Keywords

You can use the results of the syntactic dependency parse to choose the most important words for meaning recognition. In the "I want to order a pair of jeans." example, the keywords are probably "order" and "jeans."

Normally, the transitive verb plus its direct object work well for composing the intent. But in this particular example, it's a bit more complicated. You'll need to navigate the dependency tree and extract "order" (the transitive verb) and "jeans" (the object of the preposition related to the direct object "pair").

Context

Context can matter when selecting keywords, because the same phrase might have different meanings when interpreted in different applications. Suppose you have the following utterance to treat:

```
I want the newspaper delivered to my door.
```

Depending on the context, this statement might be either a request to subscribe to a newspaper or a request to deliver the issue to the door. In the first case, the keywords might be "want" and "newspaper." In the latter case, the keywords might be "delivered" and "door."

Meaning Transition

Often, people use more than one sentence to express even a very straightforward intent. As an example, consider the following discourse:

```
I already have a relaxed pair of jeans. Now I want a skinny pair.
```

In this discourse, the words reflecting the intent expressed appear in two different sentences, as illustrated in Figure 1-9.

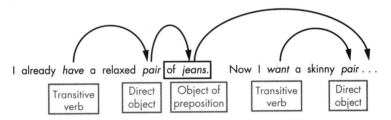

Figure 1-9: Recognizing the intent of the discourse

As you might guess, the words "want" and "jeans" best describe the intent of this discourse. The following are the general steps to finding keywords that best describe the user's intent in this particular example:

1. Within the discourse, find a transitive verb in the present tense.
2. Find the direct object of the transitive verb found in step 1.
3. If the direct object found in the previous step is a pro-form, find its antecedent in a previous sentence.

With spaCy, you can easily implement these steps programmatically. We'll describe this process in detail in Chapter 8.

Summary

In this chapter, you learned the basics of natural language processing. You now know that, unlike humans, machines use vector–based representations of words, which allow you to perform math on natural language units, including words, sentences, and documents.

You learned that word vectors are implemented in statistical models based on the neural network architecture. Then you learned about the tasks that are still left up to you as an NLP application developer.

2

THE TEXT-PROCESSING PIPELINE

Now that you understand the structure of an NLP application, it's time to see these underlying concepts in action. In this chapter, you'll install spaCy and set up your working environment. Then you'll learn about the *text-processing pipeline*, a series of basic NLP operations you'll use to determine the meaning and intent of a discourse. These operations include tokenization, lemmatization, part-of-speech tagging, syntactic dependency parsing, and named entity recognition.

Setting Up Your Working Environment

Before you start using spaCy, you need to set up a working environment by installing the following software components on your machine:

- Python 2.7 or later, or 3.4 or later
- The spaCy library
- A statistical model for spaCy

You'll need Python 2.7 or later, or 3.4 or later to use spaCy v2.0.*x*. Download it at *https://www.python.org/downloads/* and follow the instructions to set up a Python environment. Next, install spaCy in your Python environment using pip by running the following command:

```
$ pip install spacy
```

If you have more than one Python installation on your system, select the pip executable associated with the Python installation you want to use. For instance, if you want to use spaCy with Python 3.5, you'd run the following command:

```
$ pip3.5 install spacy
```

If you already have spaCy installed on your system, you might want to upgrade it to a new release. The examples in this book assume you use spaCy v2.0.*x* or later. You can verify which version of spaCy you have installed with the following command:

```
$ python -m spacy info
```

Once again, you might need to replace the python command with the command for the python executable used in your particular environment, say, python3.5. From now on, we'll use python and pip regardless of the executables your system uses.

If you decide to upgrade your installed spaCy package to the latest version, you can do this using the following pip command:

```
$ pip install -U spacy
```

Installing Statistical Models for spaCy

The spaCy installation doesn't include statistical models that you'll need when you start using the library. The statistical models contain knowledge collected about the particular language from a set of sources. You must separately download and install each model you want to use.

Several pretrained statistical models are available for different languages. For English, for example, the following models are available for download from spaCy's website: en_core_web_sm, en_core_web_md, en_core_web_lg, and en_vectors_web_lg. The models use the following naming convention: *lang_type_genre_size*. *Lang* specifies the language. *Type* indicates the model's capabilities (for example, core is a general-purpose model that includes vocabulary, syntax, entities, and vectors). *Genre* indicates the type of text the model has been trained on: web (such as Wikipedia or similar media resources) or news (news articles). *Size* indicates how large the model is: lg is large, md is medium, and sm is small. The larger the model is, the more disk space it requires. For example, the en_vectors_web_lg-2.1.0 model takes 631MB, whereas en_core_web_sm-2.1.0 takes only 10MB.

To follow along with the examples provided in this book, en_core_web_sm (the most lightweight model) will work fine. spaCy will choose it by default when you use spaCy's download command:

```
$ python -m spacy download en
```

The en shortcut link in the command instructs spaCy to download and install the best-matching default model for the English language. The best-matching model, in this context, means the one that is generated for the specified language (English in this example), a general purpose model, and the most lightweight.

To download a specific model, you must specify its name, like this:

```
$ python -m spacy download en_core_web_md
```

Once installed, you can load the model using this same shortcut you specified during the installation:

```
nlp = spacy.load('en')
```

Basic NLP Operations with spaCy

Let's begin by performing a chain of basic NLP operations that we call a processing pipeline. spaCy does all these operations for you behind the scenes, allowing you to concentrate on your application's specific logic. Figure 2-1 provides a simplified depiction of this process.

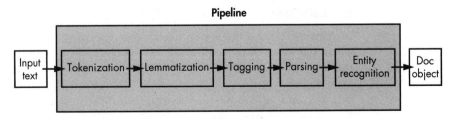

Figure 2-1: A high-level view of the processing pipeline

The processing pipeline typically includes tokenization, lemmatization, part-of-speech tagging, syntactic dependency parsing, and named entity recognition. We'll introduce each of these tasks in this section.

Tokenization

The very first action any NLP application typically performs on a text is parsing that text into *tokens*, which can be words, numbers, or punctuation marks. Tokenization is the first operation because all the other operations require you to have tokens already in place.

The following code shows the tokenization process:

```
❶ import spacy
❷ nlp = spacy.load('en')
❸ doc = nlp(u'I am flying to Frisco')
❹ print([w.text for w in doc])
```

We start by importing the spaCy library ❶ to gain access to its functionality. Then, we load a model package using the en shortcut link ❷ to create an instance of spaCy's Language class. A Language object contains the language's vocabulary and other data from the statistical model. We call the Language object nlp.

Next, we apply the object just created ❸ to a sample sentence, creating a *Doc object* instance. A Doc object is a container for a sequence of Token objects. spaCy generates it implicitly based on the text you provide it.

At this point, with just three lines of code, spaCy has generated the grammatical structure for the sample sentence. How you'll use it is entirely up to you. In this very simple example, you just print out the *text content* of each token from the sample sentence ❹.

The script outputs the sample sentence's tokens as a list:

```
['I', 'am', 'flying', 'to', 'Frisco']
```

The *text content*—the group of characters that compose the token, such as the letters "a" and "m" in the token "am"—is just one of many properties of a Token object. You can also extract various linguistic features assigned to a token, as you'll see in the following examples.

Lemmatization

A *lemma* is the base form of a token. You can think of it as the form in which the token would appear if it were listed in a dictionary. For example, the lemma for the token "flying" is "fly." *Lemmatization* is the process of reducing word forms to their lemma. The following script provides a simple example of how to do lemmatization with spaCy:

```
import spacy
nlp = spacy.load('en')
```

```
doc = nlp(u'this product integrates both libraries for downloading and
applying patches')
for token in doc:
  print(❶token.text, ❷token.lemma_)
```

The first three lines in the script are the same as those in the previous script. Recall that they import the spaCy library, load an English model using the en shortcut and create a text-processing pipeline, and apply the pipeline to a sample sentence—creating a Doc object through which you can access the grammatical structure of the sentence.

In grammar, sentence structure is the arrangement of individual words, as well as phrases and clauses in a sentence. The grammatical meaning of a sentence depends on this structural organization.

Once you have a Doc object containing the tokens from your example sentence, you iterate over those tokens in a loop, and then print out a token's text content ❶ along with its corresponding lemma ❷. This script produces the following output (I've tabulated it to make it more readable):

```
this        this
product     product
integrates  integrate
both        both
libraries   library
for         for
downloading download
and         and
applying    apply
patches     patch
```

The column on the left contains the tokens, and the column on the right contains their lemmas.

Applying Lemmatization for Meaning Recognition

Lemmatization is an important step in the task of meaning recognition. To see how, let's return to the sample sentence from the previous section:

```
I am flying to Frisco.
```

Suppose this sentence was submitted to an NLP application interacting with an online system that provides an API for booking tickets for trips. The application processes a customer's request, extracting necessary information from it and then passing on that information to the underlying API. This design might look like the one depicted in Figure 2-2.

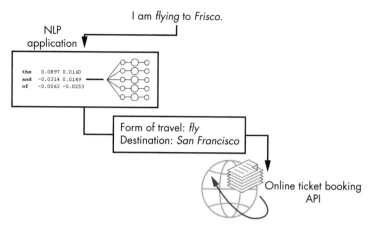

Figure 2-2: Using lemmatization in the process of extracting necessary information from a customer's request

The NLP application tries to get the following information from a customer's request: a form of travel (plane, rail, bus, and so on) and a destination. The application needs to first determine whether the customer wants an air ticket, a railway ticket, or a bus ticket. To determine this, the application searches for a word that matches one of the keywords in the predefined list. An easy way to simplify the search for these keywords is to first convert all the words in a sentence being processed to their lemmas. In that case, the predefined list of keywords will be much shorter and clearer. For example, you won't need to include all the word forms of the word fly (such as "fly," "flying," "flew," and "flown") to serve as an indicator that the customer wants an air ticket, reducing all possible variants to the base form of the word—that is, "fly."

Lemmatization also comes in handy when the application tries to determine a destination from a submitted request. There are a lot of nicknames for the globe's cities. But the system that books the tickets requires official names. Of course, the default Tokenizer that performs lemmatization won't know the difference between nicknames and official names for cities, countries, and so on. To solve this problem, you can add special case rules to an existing Tokenizer instance.

The following script illustrates how you might implement lemmatization for the destination cities example. It prints out the lemmas of the words composing the sentence.

```
import spacy
from spacy.symbols import ORTH, LEMMA
nlp = spacy.load('en')
doc = nlp(u'I am flying to Frisco')
print([w.text for w in doc])
❶ special_case = [{ORTH: u'Frisco', LEMMA: u'San Francisco'}]
❷ nlp.tokenizer.add_special_case(u'Frisco', special_case)
❸ print([w.lemma_ for w in nlp(u'I am flying to Frisco')])
```

You define a *special case* for the word `Frisco` ❶ by replacing its default lemma with `San Francisco`. Then you add this special case to the Tokenizer instance ❷. Once added, the Tokenizer instance will use this special case each time it's asked for the lemma of `Frisco`. To make sure that everything works as expected, you print out the lemmas of the words in the sentence ❸.

The script generates the following output:

```
['I', 'am', 'flying', 'to', 'Frisco']
['-PRON-', 'be', 'fly', 'to', 'San Francisco']
```

The output lists the lemmas for all words occurring in the sentence with the exception of `Frisco`, for which it lists `San Francisco`.

Part-of-Speech Tagging

A *part-of-speech tag* tells you the part-of-speech (noun, verb, and so on) of a given word in a given sentence. (Recall from Chapter 1 that a word can act as more than one part of speech depending on the context in which it appears.)

In spaCy, part-of-speech tags can include detailed information about a token. In the case of verbs, they might tell you the following features: tense (past, present, or future), aspect (simple, progressive, or perfect), person (1st, 2nd, or 3rd), and number (singular or plural).

Extracting these verb part-of-speech tags can help identify a user's intent when tokenization and lemmatization alone aren't sufficient. For instance, the lemmatization script for the ticket booking application in the preceding section won't decide how the NLP application chooses words in a sentence to compose a request to the underlying API. In a real situation, doing so might be quite complicated. For example, a customer's request might consist of more than one sentence:

```
I have flown to LA. Now I am flying to Frisco.
```

For these sentences, the results of lemmatization would be as follows:

```
['-PRON-', 'have', 'fly', 'to', 'LA', '.', 'now', '-PRON-', 'be', 'fly', 'to',
'San Francisco', '.']
```

Performing lemmatization alone isn't enough here; the application might consider the lemmas "fly" and "LA" from the first sentence as the keywords, indicating that the customer intends to fly to LA when in fact the customer intends to fly to San Francisco. Part of the problem is that lemmatization changes verbs to their infinitive forms, making it hard to know the role they play in a sentence.

This is where part-of-speech tags come into play. In English, the core parts of speech include noun, pronoun, determiner, adjective, verb, adverb, preposition, conjunction, and interjection. (See the linguistic primer in the appendix for more information about these parts of speech.) In spaCy, these same categories—plus some additional ones for symbols, punctuation marks, and others—are called *coarse-grained parts of speech* and are available as a fixed set of tags through the Token.pos (int) and Token.pos_ (unicode) attributes.

Also, spaCy offers *fine-grained parts of speech* tags that provide more detailed information about a token, covering morphological features, such as verb tenses and types of pronouns. Naturally, the list of fine-grained parts of speech contains many more tags than the coarse-grained list. The fine-grained part-of-speech tags are available as the Token.tag (int) and Token.tag_ (unicode) attributes.

Table 2-1 lists some of the common part-of-speech tags used in spaCy for English models.

Table 2-1: Some Common spaCy Part-of-Speech Tags

TAG (fine-grained part of speech)	POS (coarse-grained part of speech)	Morphology	Description
NN	NOUN	Number=sing	Noun, singular
NNS	NOUN	Number=plur	Noun, plural
PRP	PRON	PronType=prs	Pronoun, personal
PRP$	PRON	PronType=prs Poss=yes	Pronoun, possessive
VB	VERB	VerbForm=inf	Verb, base form
VBD	VERB	VerbForm=fin Tense=past	Verb, past tense
VBG	VERB	VerbForm=part Tense=pres Aspect=prog	Verb, gerund, or present participle
JJ	ADJ	Degree=pos	Adjective

NOTE   *You can find the entire list of the fine-grained part-of-speech tags used in spaCy in the "Part-of-Speech Tagging" section in the Annotation Specifications manual at* https://spacy.io/api/annotation#pos-tagging.

Tense and aspect are perhaps the most interesting properties of verbs for NLP applications. Together, they indicate a verb's reference to a position in time. For example, we use the *present tense progressive aspect* form of a verb to describe what is happening right now or what will happen in the near future. To form the present tense progressive aspect verb, you add the present tense form of the verb "to be" before an -ing verb. For example, in the sentence "I am looking into it," you add "am"—the form of the verb "to be" in the first person, present tense—before the -ing verb "looking." In this example, "am" indicates the present tense and "looking" points to the progressive aspect.

Using Part-of-Speech Tags to Find Relevant Verbs

The ticket booking application could use the fine-grained part-of speech tags available in spaCy to filter the verbs in the discourse, choosing only those that could be key to determining the customer's intent.

Before moving onto the code for this process, let's try to figure out what kind of utterances a customer might use to express their intention to book a plane ticket to, say, LA. We could start by looking at some sentences that contain the following combination of lemmas: "fly", "to", and "LA". Here are some simple options:

```
I flew to LA.
I have flown to LA.
I need to fly to LA.
I am flying to LA.
I will fly to LA.
```

Notice that although all of these sentences would include the "fly to LA" combination if reduced to lemmas, only some of them imply the customer's intent to book a plane ticket to LA. The first two definitely aren't suitable.

A quick analysis reveals that the past and past perfect forms of the verb "fly"—the tenses used in the first two sentences—don't imply the intent we're looking for. Only the infinitive and present progressive forms are suitable. The following script illustrates how to find those forms in the sample discourse:

```
import spacy
nlp = spacy.load('en')
doc = nlp(u'I have flown to LA. Now I am flying to Frisco.')
print([w.text for w in doc if ❶w.tag_ == ❷'VBG' or w.tag_ == ❸'VB'])
```

The tag_ property ❶ of a Token object contains the fine-grained part-of-speech attribute assigned to that object. You use a loop performed over the tokens composing the discourse to check whether the fine-grained part-of-speech tag assigned to a token is VB (a verb in the base, or infinitive, form) ❸ or VBG (a verb in the present progressive form) ❷.

In the sample discourse, only the verb "flying" in the second sentence meets the specified condition. So you should see the following output:

```
['flying']
```

Of course, fine-grained part-of-speech tags aren't only assigned to verbs; they're also assigned to the other parts of speech in a sentence. For example, spaCy would recognize LA and Frisco as proper nouns—nouns that are the names of individuals, places, objects, or organizations—and tag them with PROPN. If you wanted, you could add the following line of code to the previous script:

```
print([w.text for w in doc if w.pos_ == 'PROPN'])
```

Adding that code should output the following list:

```
['LA', 'Frisco']
```

The proper nouns from both sentences of the sample discourse are in the list.

Context Is Important

Fine-grained part-of-speech tags might not always be enough to determine an utterance's meaning. For this, you might still need to rely on context. As an example, consider the following utterance: "I am flying to LA." The part-of-speech tagger will assign the VBG tag to the verb "flying" in this example, because it's in the present progressive form. But because we use this verb form to describe either what is happening right now or what will happen in the near future, the utterance might mean either "I'm already in the sky, flying to LA." or "I'm going to fly to LA." When submitted to the ticket booking NLP application, the application should interpret only one of these sentences as "I need an air ticket to LA." Similarly, consider the following discourse: "I am flying to LA. In the evening, I have to be back in Frisco." This most likely implies that the speaker wants an air ticket from LA to Frisco for an evening flight. You'll find more examples about recognizing meaning based on context in "Using Context to Improve the Ticket-Booking Chatbot" on page 91.

Syntactic Relations

Now let's combine the proper nouns with the verb that the part-of-speech tagger selected earlier. Recall that the list of verbs you could potentially use to identify the intent of the discourse contains only the verb "flying" in the second sentence. How can you get the verb/proper noun pair that best describes the intent behind the discourse? A human would obviously compose the verb/proper noun pairs from words found in the same sentence. Because the verb "flown" in the first sentence doesn't meet the condition specified (remember that only infinitive and present progressive forms meet the condition), you'd be able to compose such a pair for the second sentence only: "flying, Frisco."

To handle these situations programmatically, spaCy features a syntactic dependency parser that discovers syntactic relations between individual tokens in a sentence and connects syntactically related pairs of words with a single arc.

Like lemmas and part-of-speech tags discussed in the previous sections, *syntactic dependency labels* are linguistic features that spaCy assigns to the Token objects that make up a text contained in a Doc object. For example, the dependency label dobj stands for "direct object." We could illustrate the syntactic relation it represents as an arrow arc, as shown in Figure 2-3.

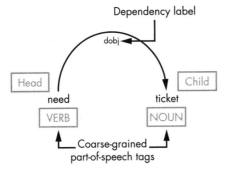

Figure 2-3: A graphical representation of a syntactic dependency arc

The `dobj` label is assigned to the word "ticket" because it's the child of the relation. A dependency label is always assigned to the child. In your script, you can determine the head of a relation using the `Token.head` attribute.

You might also want to look at the other head/child relations in the sentence, like the ones shown in Figure 2-4.

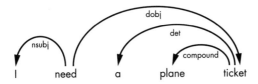

Figure 2-4: Head/child relations in an entire sentence

As you can see, the same word in a sentence can participate in several syntactic relations. Table 2-2 lists some of the most commonly used English dependency labels.

Table 2-2: Some Common Dependency Labels

Dependency label	Description
acomp	Adjectival complement
amod	Adjectival modifier
aux	Auxiliary
compound	Compound
dative	Dative
det	Determiner
dobj	Direct object
nsubj	Nominal subject
pobj	Object of preposition
ROOT	Root

The ROOT label marks the token whose head is itself. Typically, spaCy assigns it to the main verb of the sentence (the verb that is at the heart of the predicate). Every complete sentence should have a verb with the ROOT tag and a subject with the nsubj tag. The other elements are optional.

NOTE *Most of the examples in this book will assume that the submitted text is a complete sentence and use the ROOT tag to locate the sentence's main verb. Keep in mind that this won't work for every possible input.*

The following script illustrates how to access the syntactic dependency labels of the tokens in the discourse from the example in "Part-of-Speech Tagging" on page 21:

```
import spacy
nlp = spacy.load('en')
doc = nlp(u'I have flown to LA. Now I am flying to Frisco.')
for token in doc:
    print(token.text, ❶token.pos_, ❷token.dep_)
```

The script outputs the coarse-grained part-of-speech tags ❶ (see Table 2-1) and dependency labels assigned to the tokens ❷ composing the sample discourse:

```
I       PRON  nsubj
have    VERB  aux
flown   VERB  ROOT
to      ADP   prep
```

```
LA     PROPN  pobj
.      PUNCT  punct
Now    ADV    advmod
I      PRON   nsubj
am     VERB   aux
flying VERB   ROOT
to     ADP    prep
Frisco PROPN  pobj
.      PUNCT  punct
```

But what it doesn't show you is how words are related to each other in a sentence by means of the commonly called *dependency arcs* explained at the beginning of this section. To look at the dependency arcs in the sample discourse, replace the loop in the preceding script with the following one:

```
for token in doc:
    print(❶token.head.text, token.dep_, token.text)
```

The head property of a token object ❶ refers to the syntactic head of this token. When you print this line, you'll see how words in the discourse sentences are connected to each other by syntactic dependencies. If they were presented graphically, you would see an arc for each line in the following output, except for the ROOT relation. The reason is that the word to which this label is assigned is the only word in a sentence that doesn't have a head:

```
flown   nsubj   I
flown   aux     have
flown   ROOT    flown
flown   prep    to
to      pobj    LA
flown   punct   .
flying  advmod  Now
flying  nsubj   I
flying  aux     am
flying  ROOT    flying
flying  prep    to
to      pobj    Frisco
flying  punct   .
```

Looking at the earlier list of syntactic dependencies, let's try to figure out what labels point to the tokens that could potentially best describe the customer's intent: in other words, you need to find a pair that would alone appropriately describe the customer's intent.

You might be interested in the tokens marked with the ROOT and pobj dependency labels, because in this example they're key in intent recognition. As stated earlier, the ROOT label marks the main verb of the sentence, and pobj, in this example, marks the entity that—in conjunction with the verb—summarizes the meaning of the entire utterance.

The following script locates words that are assigned to those two dependency labels:

```
import spacy
nlp = spacy.load('en')
doc = nlp(u'I have flown to LA. Now I am flying to Frisco.')
❶ for sent in doc.sents:
  ❷ print([w.text for w in sent ❸if w.dep_ == 'ROOT' or w.dep_ == 'pobj'])
```

In this script, you *shred the discourse* ❶ to separate the sentences with the doc.sents property, which iterates over the sentences in the document. Shredding a text into separate sentences can be useful when you need to find, for example, certain parts of speech in each sentence of the discourse. (We'll discuss doc.sents in the next chapter, where you'll see an example of how to refer to the tokens in a document with sentence-level indices.) This allows you to create a list of potential keywords for each sentence based on specific dependency labels assigned to the tokens ❷. The filter conditions used in this example are chosen based on the examination of the syntactically related pairs generated by the previous script. In particular, you pick up the tokens with ROOT and pobj dependency labels ❸, because these tokens form the pairs you're interested in.

The script's output should look as follows:

```
['flown', 'LA']
['flying', 'Frisco']
```

In both sentence pairs, the output nouns are the ones labeled as pobj. You could use this in your ticket booking application to choose the noun that best belongs with the verb. In this case, that would be "flying," which goes with "Frisco."

This is a simplified example of information extraction using dependency labels. In the following chapters, you'll be given more sophisticated examples of how to iterate over the dependency tree of a sentence or even an entire discourse, extracting necessary pieces of information.

Try This

Now that you know how to take advantage of lemmatization, part-of-speech tags, and syntactic dependency labels, you can put them all together to do something useful. Try combining the examples from the preceding sections into a single script that correctly identifies a speaker's intent to fly to San Francisco.

Your script should generate the following output:

```
['fly', 'San Francisco']
```

To achieve this, start with the latest script from this section and enhance the conditional clause in the loop, adding the conditions to account for fine-grained part-of-speech tags, as discussed in "Part-of-Speech Tagging" on page 21. Then add the lemmatization functionality to your script, as discussed in "Lemmatization" on page 18.

Named Entity Recognition

A *named entity* is a real object that you can refer to by a proper name. It can be a person, organization, location, or other entity. Named entities are important in NLP because they reveal the place or organization the user is talking about. The following script finds named entities in the sample discourse used in the previous examples:

```
import spacy
nlp = spacy.load('en')
doc = nlp(u'I have flown to LA. Now I am flying to Frisco.')
for token in doc:
❶ if token.ent_type != 0:
        print(token.text, ❷token.ent_type_)
```

If the ent_type attribute of a token is not set to 0 ❶, then the token is a named entity. If so, you print the ent_type_ attribute of a token ❷, which contains the type of named entity in unicode. As a result, the script should output the following:

```
LA      GPE
Frisco  GPE
```

Both LA and Frisco are marked as GPE, the acronym for "geopolitical entity" and includes countries, cities, states, and other place names.

Summary

In this chapter, you set up a working environment for using spaCy. Then you learned simple scripts that illustrate how to use spaCy's features to perform the basic NLP operations for extracting important information. These operations included tokenization, lemmatization, and identifying syntactic relations between individual tokens in a sentence. The examples provided in this chapter are simplified and don't reflect real-world scenarios. To write a more sophisticated script using spaCy, you'll need to implement an algorithm to derive the necessary tokens from a dependency tree, using the linguistic features assigned to tokens. We'll return to extracting and using linguistic features in Chapter 4, and we'll cover dependency trees in detail in Chapter 6.

In the next chapter, you'll look at the key objects of spaCy's API, including containers and processing pipeline components. Also, you'll learn to use spaCy's C-level data structures and interfaces to create Python modules capable of processing large amounts of text.

3

WORKING WITH CONTAINER OBJECTS AND CUSTOMIZING SPACY

You can divide the main objects composing the spaCy API into two categories: containers (such as Tokens and Doc objects) and processing pipeline components (such as the part-of-speech tagger and named entity recognizer). This chapter explores container objects further. Using container objects and their methods, you can access the linguistic annotations that spaCy assigns to each token in a text.

You'll also learn how to customize the pipeline components to suit your needs and use Cython code to speed up time-consuming NLP tasks.

spaCy's Container Objects

A *container object* groups multiple elements into a single unit. It can be a collection of objects, like tokens or sentences, or a set of annotations related to a single object. For example, spaCy's Token object is a container for a set of annotations related to a single token in a text, such as that token's part of speech. Container objects in spaCy mimic the structure of natural language texts: a text is composed of sentences, and each sentence contains tokens.

Token, Span, and Doc, the most widely used container objects in spaCy from a user's standpoint, represent a token, a phrase or sentence, and a text, respectively. A container can contain other containers—for example, a Doc contains Tokens. In this section, we'll explore working with these container objects.

Getting the Index of a Token in a Doc Object

A Doc object contains a collection of the Token objects generated as a result of the tokenization performed on a submitted text. These tokens have indices, allowing you to access them based on their positions in the text, as shown in Figure 3-1.

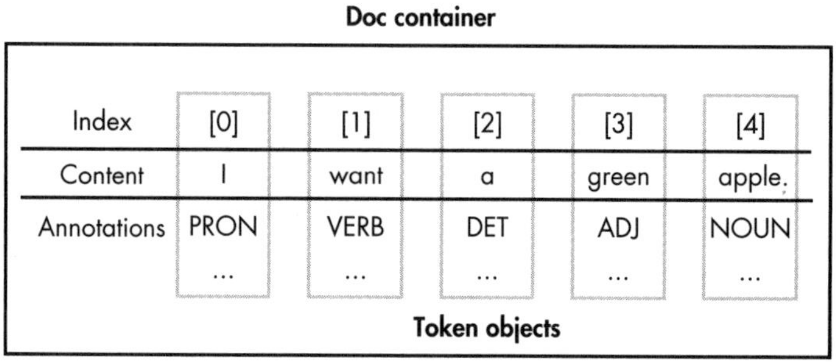

Doc container

Index	[0]	[1]	[2]	[3]	[4]
Content	I	want	a	green	apple.
Annotations	PRON	VERB	DET	ADJ	NOUN
	...	...	...	...	...

Token objects

Figure 3-1: The tokens in a Doc object

The tokens are indexed starting with 0, which makes the length of the document minus 1 the index of the end position. To shred the Doc instance into tokens, you derive the tokens into a Python list by iterating over the Doc from the start token to the end token:

```
>>> [doc[i] for i in range(len(doc))]
[A, severe, storm, hit, the, beach, .]
```

It's worth noting that we can create a Doc object using its constructor explicitly, as illustrated in the following example:

```
>>> from spacy.tokens.doc import Doc
>>> from spacy.vocab import Vocab
>>> doc = Doc(❶Vocab(), ❷words=[u'Hi', u'there'])
doc
Hi there
```

We invoke the Doc's constructor, passing it the following two parameters: a *vocab object* ❶—which is a storage container that provides vocabulary data, such as lexical types (adjective, verb, noun, and so on)—and a list of tokens to add to the Doc object being created ❷.

Iterating over a Token's Syntactic Children

Suppose we need to find the leftward children of a token in the syntactic dependency parse of a sentence. For example, we can apply this operation to a noun to obtain its adjectives, if any. We might need to do this if we want to know what adjectives are able to modify a given noun. As an example, consider the following sentence:

```
I want a green apple.
```

The diagram in Figure 3-2 highlights the syntactic dependencies of interest.

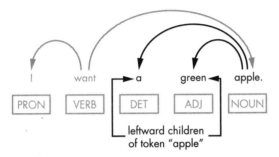

Figure 3-2: An example of leftward syntactic dependencies

To obtain the leftward syntactic children of the word "apple" in this sample sentence programmatically, we might use the following code:

```
>>> doc = nlp(u'I want a green apple.')
>>> [w for w in doc[4].lefts]
[a, green]
```

In this script, we simply iterate through the apple's children, outputting them in a list.

It's interesting to note that in this example, the leftward syntactic children of the word "apple" represent the entire sequence of the token's syntactic children. In practice, this means that we might replace Token.lefts with Token.children, which finds all of a token's syntactic children:

```
>>> [w for w in doc[4].children]
```

The result list will remain the same.

We could also use Token.rights to get a token's rightward syntactic children: in this example, the word "apple" is a rightward child of the word "want," as shown in Figure 3-1.

The doc.sents Container

Typically, the linguistic annotations assigned to a token make sense only in the context of the sentence in which the token occurs. For example, information about whether the word is a noun or a verb might apply only to the sentence in which this word is located (like the word "count," discussed in previous chapters). In such cases, it would be useful to have the ability to access the tokens in the document with sentence-level indices.

The Doc object's `doc.sents` property lets us separate a text into its individual sentences, as illustrated in the following example:

```
>>> doc = nlp(u'A severe storm hit the beach. It started to rain.')
❶ >>> for sent in doc.sents:
❷ ...    [sent[i] for i in range(len(sent))]
...
[A, severe, storm, hit, the, beach, .]
[It, started, to, rain, .]
>>>
```

We iterate over the sentences in the doc ❶, creating a separate list of tokens for each sentence ❷.

At the same time, we can still refer to the tokens in a multi-sentence text using the global, or document-level, indices, as shown here:

```
>>> [doc[i] for i in range(len(doc))]
[A, severe, storm, hit, the, beach, ., It, started, to, rain, .]
```

The ability to refer to the Token objects in a document by their sentence-level indices can be useful if, for example, we need to check whether the first word in the second sentence of the text being processed is a pronoun (say we want to figure out the connection between two sentences: the first of which contains a noun and the second of which contains a pronoun that refers to the noun):

```
>>> for i,sent in enumerate(doc.sents):
...    if i==1 and sent[0].pos_ == 'PRON':
...       print('The second sentence begins with a pronoun.')
The second sentence begins with a pronoun.
```

In this example, we use an enumerator in the for loop to distinguish the sentences by index. This allows us to filter out sentences that we're not interested in and check only the second sentence.

Identifying the first word in a sentence is a breeze, because its index is always 0. But what about the last one? For example, what if we need to find out how many sentences in the text end with a verb—(not counting any periods, of course)?

```
>>> counter = 0
>>> for sent in doc.sents:
...    if sent[len(sent)-2].pos_ == 'VERB':
...       counter+=1

>>> print(counter)
1
```

Although the lengths of sentences vary, we can easily determine the length of a given sentence using the len() function. We reduce the value of len(sent) by 2 for the following reasons: first, the indices always start at 0 and end at size-1. Second, the last token in both sentences in the sample is a period, which we need to ignore.

The doc.noun_chunks Container

A Doc object's doc.noun_chunks property allows us to iterate over the noun chunks in the document. A *noun chunk* is a phrase that has a noun as its head. For example, the previous sentence contains the following noun chunks:

```
A noun chunk
a phrase
a noun
its head
```

With doc.noun_chunks, we can extract them as follows:

```
>>> doc = nlp(u'A noun chunk is a phrase that has a noun as its head.')
>>> for chunk in doc.noun_chunks:
...     print(chunk)
```

Alternatively, we might extract noun chunks by iterating over the nouns in the sentence and finding the syntactic children for each noun to form a chunk. Earlier in "Iterating over a Token's Syntactic Children" on page 33, you saw an example of how to extract a phrase based on the syntactic dependency parse. Now let's apply this technique to the sample sentence in this example to compose noun chunks manually:

```
for token in doc:
❶ if token.pos_=='NOUN':
       chunk = ''
  ❷ for w in token.children:
       ❸ if w.pos_ == 'DET' or w.pos_ == 'ADJ':
            chunk = chunk + w.text + ' '
  ❹ chunk = chunk + token.text
       print(chunk)
```

Iterating over the tokens, we pick up only nouns ❶. Next, in the inner loop, we iterate over a noun's children ❷, picking up only the tokens that are either determiners or adjectives for the noun chunk (noun chunks can also include some other parts of speech, say, adverbs) ❸. Then we append the noun to the chunk ❹. As a result, the output of the script should be the same as in the previous example.

Try This

Notice that the words used to modify a noun (determiners and adjectives) are always the leftward syntactic children of the noun. This makes it possible to replace `Token.children` with `Token.lefts` in the previous code and then remove the check for the children to be either a determiner or an adjective, as necessary.

Rewrite the previous snippet, incorporating the changes suggested here. The resulting set of noun chunks should remain the same in your script.

The Span Object

The Span object is a slice from a Doc object. In the previous sections, you saw how to use it as a container for a sentence and a noun chunk, derived from `doc.sents` and `doc.noun_chunks`, respectively.

The Span object's usage isn't limited to being a container for sentences or noun chunks only. We can use it to contain an arbitrary set of neighboring tokens in the document by specifying a range of indices, as in the following example:

```
>>> doc=nlp('I want a green apple.')
>>> doc[2:5]
a green apple
```

The Span object contains several methods, one of the most interesting of which is `span.merge()`, which allows us to merge the span into a single token, retokenizing the document. This can be useful when the text contains names consisting of several words.

The sample sentence in the following example contains two place names consisting of several words ("Golden Gate Bridge" and "San Francisco") that we might want to group together. The default tokenization won't recognize these multi-word place names as single tokens. Look at what happens when we list the text's tokens:

```
>>> doc = nlp(u'The Golden Gate Bridge is an iconic landmark in San Francisco.')
>>> [doc[i] for i in range(len(doc))]
[The, Golden, Gate, Bridge, is, an, iconic, landmark, in, San, Francisco, .]
```

Each word and punctuation mark is its own token.
With the `span.merge()` method, we can change this default behavior:

```
>>> span = doc[1:4]
>>> lem_id = doc.vocab.strings[span.text]
>>> span.merge(lemma = lem_id)
Golden Gate Bridge
```

In this example, we create a lemma for the "Golden Gate Bridge" span, and then pass the lemma to `span.merge()` as a parameter. (To be precise, we pass on the lemma's id obtained through the `doc.vocab.string` attribute.)

Note that the `span.merge()` method doesn't merge the corresponding lemmas by default. When called without parameters, it sets the lemma of the merged token to the lemma of the first token of the span being merged. To specify the lemma we want to assign to the merged token, we pass it to `span.merge()` as the lemma parameter, as illustrated here.

Let's check whether the lemmatizer, part-of-speech tagger, and dependency parser can handle the newly created lemma correctly:

```
>>> for token in doc:
        print(token.text, token.lemma_, token.pos_, token.dep_)
```

This should produce the following output:

```
The                 the                 DET    det
Golden Gate Bridge  Golden Gate Bridge  PROPN  nsubj
is                  be                  VERB   ROOT
an                  an                  DET    det
iconic             iconic             ADJ    amod
landmark           landmark           NOUN   attr
in                 in                 ADP    prep
San                san                PROPN  compound
Francisco          francisco          PROPN  pobj
.                  .                  PUNCT  punct
```

All the attributes shown in the listing have been assigned to the "Golden Gate Bridge" token correctly.

Try This

The sentence in the preceding example also contains San Francisco, another multi-word place name that you might want to merge into a single token. To achieve this, perform the same operations as listed in the previous code snippets for the "Golden Gate Bridge" span.

When determining the start and end positions for the "San Francisco" span in the document, don't forget that the indices of the tokens located to the right of the newly created "Golden Gate Bridge" token have been shifted downward respectively.

Customizing the Text-Processing Pipeline

In the previous sections, you learned how spaCy's container objects represent linguistic units, such as a text and an individual token, allowing you to extract linguistic features associated with them. Let's now look at the objects in the spaCy API that create those containers and fill them with relevant data.

These objects are referred to as processing pipeline components. As you've already learned, a pipeline set includes—by default—a part-of-speech tagger, a dependency parser, and an entity recognizer. You can check what pipeline components are available for your nlp object like this:

```
>>> nlp.pipe_names
['tagger', 'parser', 'ner']
```

As discussed in the following sections, spaCy allows you to customize the components in your pipeline to best suit your needs.

Disabling Pipeline Components

spaCy allows you to load a selected set of pipeline components, disabling those that aren't necessary. You can do this when creating an nlp object by setting the disable parameter:

```
nlp = spacy.load('en', disable=['parser'])
```

In this example, we create a processing pipeline without a dependency parser. If we call this nlp instance on a text, the tokens won't receive dependency labels. The following example illustrates this point clearly:

```
>>> doc = nlp(u'I want a green apple.')
>>> for token in doc:
...     print(❶token.text, ❷token.pos_, ❸token.dep_)

I       PRON
want    VERB
a       DET
green   ADJ
apple   NOUN
.       PUNCT
```

We try to print out the following information for each token from the sample sentence: the text content ❶, a part-of-speech tag ❷, and a dependency label ❸. But the dependency labels don't appear.

Loading a Model Step by Step

You can perform several operations in one step with spacy.load(), which loads a model. For example, when you make this call:

```
nlp = spacy.load('en')
```

spaCy performs the following steps behind the scenes:

1. Looking at the name of the model to be loaded, spaCy identifies what Language class it should initialize. In this example, spaCy creates an English class instance with shared vocabulary and other language data.
2. spaCy iterates over the processing pipeline names, creates corresponding components, and adds them to the processing pipeline.
3. spaCy loads the model data from disk and makes it available to the Language class instance.

These implementation details are hidden by spacy.load(), which in most cases saves you effort and time. But sometimes, you might need to implement these steps explicitly to have fine-grained control over the process. For example, you might need to load a custom component to the processing pipeline.

The component could print some information about the Doc object in the pipeline, such as the number of tokens or the presence or absence of certain parts of speech.

As usual, more fine-grained control requires you to provide more information. First, rather than specifying a shortcut, you'll need to obtain the actual model name so you can get the path to the model package.

You can identify the full name of the model as follows:

```
>>> print(nlp.meta['lang'] + '_' + nlp.meta['name'])
en_core_web_sm
```

The `nlp.meta` attribute used in this code is a dictionary that contains the metadata of the loaded model. What you need in this example is the model's language and the model's name.

Now that you know the model's name, you can find its location in your system by using the get_package_path utility function:

```
>>> from spacy import util
>>> util.get_package_path('en_core_web_sm')
PosixPath('/usr/local/lib/python3.5/site-packages/en_core_web_sm')
```

The path specified in this code might be different on your machine, depending on your Python installation directory. Regardless, this is not the full path. You'll need to append one more folder to it. The name of this folder is composed of the model name and the model version appended to it. (This is where the model package is located.) You can determine its name as follows:

```
>>> print(nlp.meta['lang'] + '_' + nlp.meta['name'] + '-' + nlp.
meta['version'])
en_core_web_sm-2.0.0
```

You might also want to look at the list of pipeline components used with the model. (It's important to know what components are supported in the context of the model and therefore can be loaded to the pipeline.) You can obtain this information via the `nlp.meta` attribute's `'pipeline'` field, as shown here (or via the `nlp.pipe_names` attribute introduced in the beginning of "Customizing the Text-Processing Pipeline" on page 37):

```
>>> nlp.meta['pipeline']
['tagger', 'parser', 'ner']
```

With this information, we can create a script that implements the steps provided at the beginning of this section:

```
>>> lang = 'en'
>>> pipeline = ['tagger', 'parser', 'ner']
>>> model_data_path = '/usr/local/lib/python3.5/site-packages/en_core_web_sm/
en_core_web_sm-2.0.0'
❶ >>> lang_cls = spacy.util.get_lang_class(lang)
```

```
    >>> nlp = lang_cls()
❷ >>> for name in pipeline:
❸ ...     component = nlp.create_pipe(name)
❹ ...     nlp.add_pipe(component)
❺ >>> nlp.from_disk(model_data_path)
```

In this script, we use `spacy.util.get_lang_class()` ❶ to load a Language class. Which class we load depends on the two-letter language code specified as the parameter. In this example, we load English. Next, in a loop ❷, we create ❸ and add ❹ the pipeline components to the processing pipeline. Then we load a model from disk, specifying the path to it used on your machine ❺.

Looking at the code in this script, it might seem that the pipeline components become functional once we've added them to the processing pipeline. Actually, we can't use them until we load the model data, so if we omit the last line of code in the script, we won't even be able to create a Doc object using this nlp instance.

Customizing the Pipeline Components

By customizing pipeline components, you can best meet the needs of your application. For example, suppose you want your model's named entity recognizer system to recognize the word Festy as a city district. By default, it recognizes it as an organization, as illustrated in the following example:

```
>>> doc = nlp(u'I need a taxi to Festy.')
>>> for ent in doc.ents:
...   print(ent.text, ent.label_)

Festy ORG
```

The label `ORG` stands for companies, agencies, and other institutions. But you want to make the entity recognizer classify it as an entity of type `DISTRICT` instead.

The entity recognizer component is implemented in the spaCy API as the `EntityRecognizer` class. Using this class's methods, you can initialize an instance of `ner` and then apply it to a text. In most cases, you don't need to perform these operations explicitly; spaCy does it for you under the hood when you create an nlp object and then create a Doc object, respectively.

But when you want to update the named entity recognition system of an existing model with your own examples, you'll need to work with some of the ner object's methods explicitly.

In the following example, you'll first have to add a new label called `DISTRICT` to the list of supported entity types. Then you need to create a training example, which is what you'll show the entity recognizer so it will learn what to apply the `DISTRICT` label to. The simplest implementation of the preparation steps might look as follows:

```
LABEL = 'DISTRICT'
TRAIN_DATA = [
```

```
❶ ('We need to deliver it to Festy.', {
      ❷ 'entities': [(25, 30, 'DISTRICT')]
    }),
❸ ('I like red oranges', {
       'entities': []
    })
]
```

For simplicity, this training set contains just two training samples (typically, you need to provide many more). Each training sample includes a sentence that might or might not contain an entity (or entities) to which the new entity label should be assigned ❶. If there is an entity in the sample, you specify its start and end position ❷. The second sentence in the training set doesn't contain the word Festy at all ❸. This is due to the way the training process is organized. Chapter 10 covers the details of this process in more depth.

Your next step is to add a new entity label DISTRICT to the entity recognizer: but before you can do this, you must get the instance of the ner pipeline component. You can do this as follows:

```
ner = nlp.get_pipe('ner')
```

Once you have a ner object, you can add a new label to it using the ner .add_label() method, as shown here:

```
ner.add_label(LABEL)
```

Another action you need to take before you can start training the entity recognizer is to disable the other pipes to make sure that only the entity recognizer will be updated during the training process:

```
nlp.disable_pipes('tagger')
nlp.disable_pipes('parser')
```

Then you can start training the entity recognizer using the training samples in the TRAIN_DATA list created earlier in this section:

```
optimizer = nlp.entity.create_optimizer()
import random

for i in range(25):
    random.shuffle(TRAIN_DATA)
    for text, annotations in TRAIN_DATA:
        nlp.update([text], [annotations], sgd=optimizer)
```

During training, the sample examples are shown to the model in a loop, in random order, to efficiently update the underlying model's data and avoid any generalizations based on the order of training examples. The execution will take a while.

Once the preceding code has successfully completed, you can test how the updated optimizer recognizes the token Festy:

```
>>> doc = nlp(u'I need a taxi to Festy.')
>>> for ent in doc.ents:
...   print(ent.text, ent.label_)
...
Festy DISTRICT
```

According to the output, it works correctly.

Keep in mind that the updates you just made will be lost when you close this Python interpreter session. To address this problem, the Pipe class—the parent of the EntityRecognizer class and other pipeline components classes—has the to_disk() method, which allows you to serialize the pipe to disk:

```
>>> ner.to_disk('/usr/to/ner')
```

Now you can load the updated component to a new session with the from_disk() method. To make sure it works, close your current interpreter session, start a new one, and then run the following code:

```
    >>> import spacy
    >>> from spacy.pipeline import EntityRecognizer
❶  >>> nlp = spacy.load('en', disable=['ner'])
❷  >>> ner = EntityRecognizer(nlp.vocab)
❸  >>> ner.from_disk('/usr/to/ner')
❹  >>> nlp.add_pipe(ner)
```

You load the model, disabling its default ner component ❶. Next, you create a new ner instance ❷ and then load it with the data from disk ❸. Then you add the ner component to the processing pipeline ❹.

Now you can test it, like this:

```
>>> doc = nlp(u'We need to deliver it to Festy.')
>>> for ent in doc.ents:
...   print(ent.text, ent.label_)

Festy DISTRICT
```

As you can see, the entity recognizer labels the name Festy correctly.

Although I've shown you how to customize the named entity recognizer only, you can also customize the other pipeline components in a similar way.

Using spaCy's C-Level Data Structures

Even with spaCy, NLP operations that involve processing large amounts of text can be very time-consuming. For example, you might need to compose a list of the adjectives most appropriate for a certain noun, and to do this, you'll have to examine a large amount of text. If processing speed is critical to your application, spaCy allows you to take advantage of Cython's C-level data structures and interfaces. Cython is one of the languages in which spaCy is written (the other one is Python). Because it's a superset of Python, Cython considers almost all Python code valid Cython code. In addition to Python's functionality, Cython allows you to natively call C functions and declare fast C types, enabling the compiler to generate very efficient code. You might want to use Cython to speed up time-consuming text processing operations.

spaCy's core data structures are implemented as Cython objects, and spaCy's public API allows you to access those structures. For details, refer to the Cython Architecture page in the documentation at *https://spacy.io/api /cython/*.

How It Works

To use Cython code with spaCy, you must turn it into a Python extension module that you can then import into your program, as illustrated in Figure 3-3.

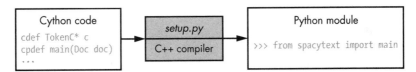

Figure 3-3: Building a Python extension module from a Cython script

You can do this by saving Cython code in a *.pyx* file and then running a *setup.py* Python script that first converts Cython code into corresponding C or C++ code and then invokes a C or C++ compiler. The script generates the Python extension module.

Preparing Your Working Environment and Getting Text Files

Before you can start building Cython code, you need to install Cython on your machine and obtain a large text file to work with.

Install Cython on your machine using pip:

```
pip install Cython
```

Next, to simulate a time-consuming task and measure performance, you'll need a large text file. For this, you can use a *Wikipedia dump file*, which contains a set of pages wrapped in XML. Wikipedia dump files are available for download at *https://dumps.wikimedia.org/enwiki/latest/*. Scroll down to the *enwiki-latest-pages-articles*.xml-*.bz2* files and choose one that is large enough for your tests. But don't choose one that is too large unless you want to spend hours waiting for your machine to complete your test code. A dump file of 10–100MB should be appropriate.

Once you've downloaded the file, extract raw text from it with a tool like *gensim.corpora.wikicorpus* (*https://radimrehurek.com/gensim/corpora/wikicorpus .html*), which is designed specifically for constructing a text corpus from a Wikipedia database dump.

Your Cython Script

Now let's write a Cython script that analyzes the text file. For simplicity, suppose all you want to do is count the number of personal pronouns in the submitted text. That means you need to count the number of tokens with the PRP part-of-speech tag assigned to them.

WARNING   *As stated in the documentation, C-level methods intended for use from Cython are designed for speed over safety. Mistakes in the code might cause the execution to crash abruptly.*

In a directory in your local filesystem, create a file called *spacytext.pyx* and insert the following code into it:

```
from cymem.cymem cimport Pool
from spacy.tokens.doc cimport Doc
from spacy.structs cimport TokenC
from spacy.typedefs cimport hash_t

❶ cdef struct DocStruct:
      TokenC* c
      int length

❷ cdef int counter(DocStruct* doc, hash_t tag):
      cdef int cnt = 0
      for c in doc.c[:doc.length]:
          if c.tag == tag:
              cnt += 1
      return cnt

❸ cpdef main(Doc mydoc):
      cdef int cnt
      cdef Pool mem = Pool()
      cdef DocStruct* doc_ptr = <DocStruct*>mem.alloc(1, sizeof(DocStruct))
      doc_ptr.c = mydoc.c
      doc_ptr.length = mydoc.length
      tag = mydoc.vocab.strings.add('PRP')
      cnt = counter(doc_ptr, tag)
      print(doc_ptr.length)
      print(cnt)
```

We start with a set of cimport statements to import necessary Cython modules, mostly from the spaCy library.

Then we define the Cython struct DocStruct as the container for the text being processed and the TokenC* variable ❶, a pointer to a TokenC struct used in spaCy as the data container for the Token object.

Next, we define a Cython function counter ❷ that counts the number of personal pronouns in the text.

NOTE *The* cdef *functions won't be available in the Python code that imports the module. If you want to create a function that will be visible to Python and to take advantage of C-level data structures and interfaces at the same time, you need to declare that function as* cpdef.

Finally, we define a cpdef Cython/Python main function ❸ that we can use in Python.

Building a Cython Module

Unlike Python, you must compile Cython code. You can do this in several ways, the best of which is to write a distutils/setuptools *setup.py* Python script. Create a *setup.py* file in the same directory as your Cython script. Your *setup.py* file should include the following code:

```
  from distutils.core import setup
  from Cython.Build import cythonize
❶ import numpy

  setup(name='spacy text app',
❷   ext_modules=cythonize("spacytext.pyx", language="c++"),
❸   include_dirs=[numpy.get_include()]
      )
```

This is a regular distutils/setuptools *setup.py* script except for two additions related to the example we're working with. First, we import numpy ❶ and then explicitly specify where to find the *.h* files of the library ❸. We do this to avoid the *numpy/arrayobject.h* compilation error that occurs in some systems. We use the other setup option, language = "c++" ❷ to instruct the setup process to employ a C++ compiler rather than performing C compilation, which is the default.

Now that we have the setup script, you can build your Cython code. You can do this from within a system terminal, as follows:

```
python setup.py build_ext --inplace
```

A bunch of messages will display during the compilation process. Some of them might be warnings, but they're rarely critical. For example, you might see this message, which is not critical for the process:

```
#warning "Using deprecated NumPy API ...
```

Testing the Module

After the compilation completes successfully, the spacytext module will be added to your Python environment. To test the newly created module, open a Python session and run the following command:

```
>>> from spacytext import main
```

If it displays no errors, you can enter the following commands (this assumes your text data is in a *test.txt* file):

```
>>> import spacy
>>> nlp = spacy.load('en')
❶ >>> f= open("test.txt","rb")
>>> contents =f.read()
❷ >>> doc = nlp(contents[:100000].decode('utf8'))
❸ >>> main(doc)
21498
216
```

You open the file in which you have text data for this example in binary mode to obtain a bytes object ❶. If the file is too big, you can pick up only part of its content when creating a Doc object ❷. Once you've created the Doc object, you can test the spacytext module you just created with Cython, invoking its main() function ❸.

The first figure in the output generated by the spacytext.main() function shows the total number of tokens found in the submitted text. The second figure is the number of personal pronouns found in this same text.

Summary

In this chapter, you looked at the most important of spaCy's container objects. You also learned how to customize your text-processing pipeline and use spaCy's C-level data structures and interfaces from Cython.

4

EXTRACTING AND USING LINGUISTIC FEATURES

In the previous chapters, you learned how to access linguistic features, such as part-of-speech tags, syntactic dependencies, and named entities, as part of the text processing pipeline. This chapter will show you how to use part-of-speech tags and syntactic dependency labels to extract and generate text, allowing you to build question-asking chatbots, locate specific phrases in a text, and more.

Almost every NLP application needs to extract specific information from a text and generate new text that is relevant to a particular situation. For example, a chatbot must be able carry on a conversation with a user, which means it must be able to identify specific parts of a user's text and then generate its own appropriate response. Let's look at how to do all of that using linguistic features.

Extracting and Generating Text with Part-of-Speech Tags

Part-of-speech tags can help you retrieve specific kinds of information from a text, and they can also help you generate entirely new sentences based on a submitted one. In this section, we'll introduce you to some new part-of-speech tags, write a script that finds phrases describing amounts of money, and transform statements into questions. For a list of common part-of-speech tags used in spaCy for English models, refer to Table 2-1 on page 22.

Numeric, Symbolic, and Punctuation Tags

In addition to part-of-speech tags for nouns, verbs, and other words in a sentence, spaCy has tags for symbols, numbers, and punctuation marks. Let's look at these by processing the following sentence:

```
The firm earned $1.5 million in 2017.
```

To begin, let's extract the coarse-grained part-of-speech features from the tokens in the sentence to see how spaCy distinguishes between different part-of-speech categories. We can do this with the following script:

```
>>> import spacy
>>> nlp = spacy.load('en')
>>> doc = nlp(u"The firm earned $1.5 million in 2017.")
>>> for token in doc:
...     print(token.text, ❶token.pos_, ❷spacy.explain(token.pos_))
...
```

We create a Doc object for the submitted sentence and then output the coarse-grained part-of-speech tags ❶. We also use the spacy.explain() function, which returns a description for a given linguistic feature ❷.

The output should look as follows:

```
The     DET   determiner
firm    NOUN  noun
earned  VERB  verb
$       SYM   symbol
1.5     NUM   numeral
million NUM   numeral
in      ADP   adposition
2017    NUM   numeral
.       PUNCT punctuation
```

Notice that the coarse-grained tagger distinguishes numerals, symbols, and punctuation marks as individual categories. As you can see, it even recognizes "million" spelled out.

Now, for the sake of comparison, let's output both coarse-grained and fine-grained part-of-speech tags for this sample sentence along with a description column for the fine-grained tags:

```
>>> for token in doc:
...     print(token.text, token.pos_, token.tag_, spacy.explain(token.tag_))
```

The output should look as follows:

```
The     DET   DT   determiner
firm    NOUN  NN   noun, singular
earned  VERB  VBD  verb, past tense
$       SYM   $    symbol, currency
1.5     NUM   CD   cardinal number
million NUM   CD   cardinal number
in      ADP   IN   conjunction, subordinating or preposition
2017    NUM   CD   cardinal number
.       PUNCT .    punctuation mark, sentence closer
```

The second and third columns contain the coarse-grained and fine-grained part-of-speech tags, respectively. The fourth column gives descriptions of the fine-grained tags provided in the third column.

The fine-grained tagging divides each category into subcategories. For example, the coarse-grained category SYM (symbols) has three fine-grained subcategories. These are $ for currency symbols, # for the number sign, and SYM for all the other symbols, such as +, −, ×, ÷, =. This sub-dividing can be useful when you need to distinguish between different types of symbols. For example, you might be processing articles about math and want your script to recognize symbols commonly found in math formulas. Or you might be writing a script that needs to recognize currency symbols in financial reports.

NOTE   *Because spaCy's part-of-speech tagger relies on a token's context to generate its label, you might get different labels for tokens used in unusual contexts.*

Now let's look at how we can take advantage of these specific part-of-speech tags to extract and generate text.

Extracting Descriptions of Money

Suppose you're developing an application for processing financial reports that must extract necessary pieces of information from long, boring texts. In practice, financial reports can be quite large, but all you really need are the figures. In particular, you're interested in phrases that refer to an amount of money and start with a currency symbol. For example, your script should pick out the phrase "$1.5 million" from the previous sample sentence, but not "2017".

The following script illustrates how you might extract this phrase from the sentence, relying on the tokens' part-of-speech tags only. You can save this script to a file and then run it or execute the code from within a Python session:

```
import spacy
nlp = spacy.load('en')
doc = nlp(u"The firm earned $1.5 million in 2017.")
phrase = ''
❶ for token in doc:
  ❷ if token.tag_ == '$':
        phrase = token.text
        i = token.i+1
      ❸ while doc[i].tag_ == 'CD':
            phrase += doc[i].text + ' '
            i += 1
      ❹ break
phrase = phrase[:-1]
print(phrase)
```

We iterate over the sentence's tokens ❶, searching for a token whose fine-grained part-of-speech tag is $ ❷. This tag indicates a currency symbol, and it typically starts a phrase that refers to an amount of money. Once we find a currency symbol, we start composing the phrase by checking whether the tokens that follow the currency symbol in the sentence are numbers. To do this, we implement a while loop in which we pick up the tokens located to the right of the currency symbol and check them for the CD tag, which is the cardinal number fine-grained part-of-speech-tag ❸. When we reach a nonnumeric token, we quit the while loop and break the for loop ❹ that iterates over the sentence's tokens.

When we run the script, the output should look as follows:

```
$1.5 million
```

This is exactly the kind of output we are looking for.

Keep in mind that a currency symbol assigned to the $ fine-grained part-of-speech tag might not necessarily be "$". The part-of-speech tag might label other common currency symbols, such as £ and €. For example, the preceding script would recognize the phrase "£1.500.000".

Try This

We wrote this script to extract a single phrase referring to an amount of money from the submitted sentence. Once the script finds the phrase, it completes its execution. But in practice, you might have a sentence that has more than one such phrase, as in the following example: "The firm earned $1.5 million in 2017, in comparison with $1.2 million in 2016."

Modify the script so it extracts every phrase that refers to an amount of money within a sentence. To accomplish this, remove the break statement to prevent the loop from ending after it finds the first occurrence of the phrase of interest. Then move the code that's responsible for preparing and printing a found phrase (the last two lines of the script) into the loop, so you can invoke these two lines for every phrase of interest found in the submitted sentence.

Turning Statements into Questions

Suppose your NLP application must be able to generate a question from a submitted statement. For example, one way chatbots maintain conversations with the user is by asking the user a confirmatory question. When a user says, "I am sure," the chatbot might ask something like, "Are you really sure?" To do this, the chatbot must be able to generate a relevant question.

Let's say the user's submitted sentence is this:

```
I can promise it is worth your time.
```

This sentence contains several verbs and pronouns, each with different morphologies. To see this more clearly, let's look at the part-of-speech tags spaCy assigned to the tokens in this sentence:

```
>>> doc = nlp(u"I can promise it is worth your time.")
>>> for token in doc:
...     print(token.text, token.pos_, token.tag_)
...
```

We print the tokens, their coarse-grained part-of-speech tags, and their fine-grained part-of-speech-tags, producing the following output:

```
I        PRON   PRP
can      VERB   MD
promise  VERB   VB
it       PRON   PRP
is       VERB   VBZ
worth    ADJ    JJ
your     ADJ    PRP$
time     NOUN   NN
.        PUNCT  .
```

From the fine-grained part-of-speech tags, you can distinguish between the morphological categories of the verbs and pronouns present in the sentence. For example, the fine-grained part-of-speech tag PRP marks personal pronouns and PRP$ marks possessive pronouns, allowing you to distinguish between these two types of pronouns programmatically. We'll need this information when working on this example.

A confirmatory question to the sentence discussed here might be as follows (another statement would require another confirmatory question, of course):

```
Can you really promise it is worth my time?
```

From a human perspective, forming this question from the statement looks pretty straightforward: you change the order of some words, alter the pronouns accordingly, and add the adverbial modifier "really" to the main verb (the one that comes right after the subject). But how can you accomplish all these operations programmatically?

Let's look at some part-of-speech tags. In the sample sentence, the verbs involved in forming the question are "can" and "promise". The fine-grained part-of-speech tags mark the first one, "can", as a modal auxiliary verb and the second one as a verb in the base form. Notice that in the preceding confirmatory question, the modal auxiliary verb has switched places with the personal pronoun, a process called *inversion*. We'll have to implement this in the script.

When it comes to the pronouns, the chatbot should follow a pattern common to regular conversations. Table 4-1 summarizes the use of pronouns in such an application.

Table 4-1: The Use of Pronouns in a Chatbot

	Personal pronouns	Possessive pronouns
chatbot	I, me	my, mine
user	you	your, yours

In other words, a chatbot refers to itself as "I" or "me," and it refers to a user as "you."

The following steps outline what we need to do to generate a question from the original statement:

1. Change the order of words in the original sentence from "subject + modal auxiliary verb + infinitive verb" to "modal auxiliary verb + subject + infinitive verb."

2. Replace the personal pronoun "I" (the sentence's subject) with "you."

3. Replace the possessive pronoun "your" with "my."

4. Place the adverbial modifier "really" before the verb "promise" to emphasize the latter.

5. Replace the punctuation mark "." with "?" at the end of the sentence.

The following script implements these steps:

```
import spacy
nlp = spacy.load('en')
doc = nlp(u"I can promise it is worth your time.")
sent = ''
for i,token in enumerate(doc):
❶ if token.tag_ == 'PRP' and doc[i+1].tag_ == 'MD' and doc[i+2].tag_ == 'VB':
    ❷ sent =  doc[i+1].text.capitalize() + ' ' + doc[i].text
       sent = sent + ' ' + ❸doc[i+2:].text
    ❹ break
#By now, you should have: 'Can I promise it is worth your time.'
```

```
  #Retokenization
❺ doc=nlp(sent)
  for i,token in enumerate(doc):
  ❻ if token.tag_ == 'PRP' and token.text == 'I':
        sent = doc[:i].text + ' you ' +  doc[i+1:].text
        break
  #By now, you should have: 'Can you promise it is worth your time.'
  doc=nlp(sent)
  for i,token in enumerate(doc):
  ❼ if token.tag_ == 'PRP$' and token.text == 'your':
        sent = doc[:i].text + ' my ' +  doc[i+1:].text
        break
  #By now, you should have: 'Can you promise it is worth my time.'
  doc=nlp(sent)
  for i,token in enumerate(doc):
    if token.tag_ == 'VB':
    ❽ sent = doc[:i].text + ' really ' +  doc[i:].text
        break
  #By now, you should have: 'Can you really promise it is worth my time.'
  doc=nlp(sent)
❾ sent = doc[:len(doc)-1].text + '?'
  #Finally, you should have: 'Can you really promise it is worth my time?'
  print(sent)
```

We perform the first four steps in separate for loops. First, we iterate over the tokens in the sentence and change the order of the subject and verb to make the sentence a question. In this example, we're looking for the modal auxiliary verb (tagged MD) that follows a personal pronoun and is followed by an infinitive verb ❶. Once we find this sequence of words, we move the modal auxiliary verb immediately before the personal pronoun, placing it at the beginning of the sentence ❷.

To compose a new sentence, we use a technique known in Python as *slicing* that allows us to extract a subsequence from a sequence object, such as a string or a list, by specifying the start and end indices. In this case, we can apply slicing to a Doc object to extract a given subsequence of tokens from it. For example, slice doc[2:] will contain the doc's tokens starting from the token at index 2 through the end of the doc, which in this case, is "promise it is worth your time." ❸. Once we move the modal verb to a new position, we exit the for loop ❹.

You might wonder why we don't just use the personal pronoun and auxiliary modal verb's indices to perform inversion. Because we know the personal pronoun is at index 0 and the modal verb is at index 1, why do we have to use a loop that iterates over the entire set of tokens to find the modal verb's position? Won't the verb always follow the subject and so be the second word in the sentence?

The fact is that a sentence doesn't always start with the subject. For example, what if the sentence were "Sure enough, I can promise it is worth your time."? In that case, the script would know to omit the first two words and start processing with the subject.

As a result of the inversion, we get the new sentence as a string. To make this sentence available for further processing, we need to obtain a Doc object for it ❺.

Next, we create a new for loop that will replace the personal pronoun "I" with the personal pronoun "you." To do this, we search for personal pronouns (tagged PRP). If the personal pronoun is "I," we replace it with "you" ❻. Then we quit the for loop.

We repeat this process to replace the possessive pronoun "your" with "my" by searching for the PRP$ tag ❼. Then, in a new for loop, we find a verb in the infinitive form and insert the adverbial modifier "really" before it ❽.

Finally, we replace the sentence's period with a question mark. This is the only step where we don't need to use a loop. The reason is that in all possible sentences, the period and the question mark go at the end of a sentence, so we can reliably find them using their indices with len(doc)-1 ❾.

When we run this code, we should get the following output:

```
Can you really promise it is worth my time?
```

This script is a good start, but it won't work with every submitted statement. For example, the statement might contain a personal pronoun other than "I," but our script doesn't explicitly check for that. Also, some sentences don't contain auxiliary verbs, like the sentence "I love eating ice cream." In those cases, we'd have to use the word "do" to form the question instead of a word like "can" or "should," like this: "Do you really love eating ice cream?" But if the sentence contains the verb "to be," as in the sentence "I am sleepy," we'd have to move that verb to the front, like this: "Are you sleepy?"

A real implementation of this chatbot would have to be able to choose the appropriate option for a submitted sentence. You'll see a "do" example in "Deciding What Question a Chatbot Should Ask" on page 56.

Try This

Examining the script from "Turning Statements into Questions", you might notice that some blocks of code in it look very similar, containing repetitive operations. In every step, you make a replacement in the sentence and then re-tokenize it. That means you might try to generalize the code, putting repetitive operations in a single function.

Before writing such a function, take some time to understand what parameters it will need to take to perform the text-manipulation operations you see in the script. In particular, you'll need to explicitly specify what token you're searching for and what operation you want to perform on it by either replacing it with another token or adding a token before it.

Once you define this function, you can write the main code that invokes it, implementing the same functionality as the original script.

Using Syntactic Dependency Labels in Text Processing

As you learned in "Extracting and Generating Text with Part-of-Speech Tags" on page 48, part-of-speech tags are a powerful tool for smart text processing. But in practice, you might need to know more about a sentence's tokens to process it intelligently.

For example, you might need to know whether a personal pronoun is the subject of a sentence or a grammatical object. Sometimes, this task is easy. The personal pronouns "I," "he," "she," "they," and "we" will almost always be the subject. When used as an object, "I" turns into "me," as in "A postman brought me a letter."

But this might not be as clear when it comes to some other personal pronouns, such as "you" or "it," which look the same whether they're used as subjects or objects. Consider the following two sentences: "I know you. You know me." In the first sentence, "you" is the direct object of the verb "know." In the second sentence, "you" is the verb's subject.

Let's solve this problem using syntactic dependency labels and part-of-speech tags. Then we'll apply syntactic dependency labels to build a better version of the question-asking chatbot.

Distinguishing Subjects from Objects

To programmatically determine the role of a pronoun like "you" or "it" in a given sentence, you need to check the dependency label assigned to it. By using part-of-speech tags in conjunction with dependency labels, you can get much more information about the tokens of a sentence.

Let's return to the sentence in the previous example and look at the results of the dependency parsing performed on it:

```
>>> doc = nlp(u"I can promise it is worth your time.")
>>> for token in doc:
...    print(token.text, token.pos_, token.tag_, token.dep_, spacy.explain(token.dep_))
```

We extract the part-of-speech tags, the dependency labels, and the description for the dependency labels:

```
I        PRON  PRP   nsubj     nominal subject
can      VERB  MD    aux       auxiliary
promise  VERB  VB    ROOT      None
it       PRON  PRP   nsubj     nominal subject
is       VERB  VBZ   ccomp     clausal complement
worth    ADJ   JJ    acomp     adjectival complement
your     ADJ   PRP$  poss      possession modifier
time     NOUN  NN    npadvmod  noun phrase as adverbial modifier
.        PUNCT .     punct     punctuation
```

The second and third columns contain the coarse-grained and fine-grained part-of-speech tags, respectively. The fourth column contains the dependency labels, and the fifth column contains descriptions for those dependency labels.

Combining part-of-speech tags and dependency labels can give you a better picture of the grammatical role of each token in a sentence—more so than just part-of-speech tags or dependency labels alone. For instance, in this example, the part-of-speech tag VBZ assigned to the token "is" indicates a verb in the third person singular present, whereas the dependency label ccomp, assigned to the same token, indicates that "is" is a *clausal complement* (a dependent clause with an internal subject). In this example, "is" is a clausal complement of the verb "promise" with the internal subject "it."

To figure out the role of "you" in "I know you. You know me.", we'd check the following list of part-of-speech tags and dependency labels assigned to the tokens:

```
I      PRON   PRP   nsubj   nominal subject
know   VERB   VBP   ROOT    None
you    PRON   PRP   dobj    direct object
.      PUNCT  .     punct   punctuation
You    PRON   PRP   nsubj   nominal subject
know   VERB   VBP   ROOT    None
me     PRON   PRP   dobj    direct object
.      PUNCT  .     Punct   punctuation
```

In both cases, "you" is assigned the same part-of-speech tags: PRON and PRP (coarse-grained and fine-grained, respectively). But the two cases have different dependency labels: dobj in the first sentence and nsubj in the second.

Deciding What Question a Chatbot Should Ask

Sometimes, you might need to navigate a sentence's dependency tree to extract necessary information. For example, consider the following conversation between a chatbot and its user:

```
User: I want an apple.
Bot: Do you want a red apple?
User: I want a green apple.
Bot: Why do you want a green one?
```

The chatbot is able to continue the conversation by asking questions. But notice that the presence or absence of an adjectival modifier for the noun "apple" plays a key role in deciding what type of question it should ask.

There are two basic types of questions in English: yes/no questions and information questions. Yes/no questions, like the one we generated in the example discussed in "Turning Statements into Questions" on page 51, can have only two possible answers: yes or no. To form a question of this type, you place a modal auxiliary verb before the subject and the main verb after the subject. For example: "Could you modify it?"

Information questions are supposed to be answered with more information than just yes or no. They begin with a question word, such as "what," "where," "when," "why," or "how." After the question word, the process of forming an information question is the same as for yes/no questions. For example: "What do you think about it?"

In the first case in the preceding apple example, the chatbot asks a yes/no question. In the second case, when the user modifies the noun "apple" with the adjective "green," the chatbot asks an information question.

The flowchart in Figure 4-1 summarizes this approach.

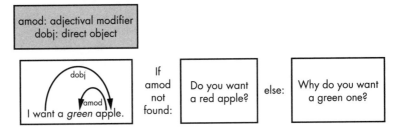

Figure 4-1: The presence of a modifier in the input sentence determines what question the chatbot asks.

The following script simply analyzes a submitted sentence to decide what kind of question to ask and then forms the proper question. We'll walk through the code in separate sections, but you should save the entire program in a single file called *question.py*.

Begin by importing the sys module, which provides functionality for accepting a sentence for processing as an argument:

```
import spacy
import sys
```

This is an improvement from the previous scripts where we hardcoded the sentence to analyze. Now users can submit their own sentences as input.

Next, we define a function that recognizes and extracts any noun chunk that is a direct object from a submitted doc. For example, if you submit a doc that contains the sentence "I want a green apple.", it will return the chunk "a green apple":

```
def find_chunk(doc):
  chunk = ''
❶ for i,token in enumerate(doc):
  ❷ if token.dep_ == 'dobj':
    ❸ shift = len([w for w in token.children])
    ❹ #print([w for w in token.children])
    ❺ chunk = doc[i-shift:i+1]
      break
  return chunk
```

We iterate over the tokens in the submitted sentence ❶ and look for the one that acts as a direct object by checking whether its dependency tag is dobj ❷. In the sentence "I want a green apple.", The direct object is the noun "apple." Once we've found the direct object, we need to determine its syntactic children ❸, because they form the chunk that we'll use to decide what kind of question to ask. For debugging purposes, we might also want to look at the children of the direct object ❹.

To extract the chunk, we slice the Doc object, calculating the start and the end indices of the slice as follows: the start index is the index of the direct object minus the number of its syntactic children. As you might guess, this is the index of the leftmost child. The end index is the index of the direct object plus one, so the last token included in the chunk is the direct object ❺.

For simplicity, the algorithm implemented in this script assumes that a direct object has only leftward children. In fact, this isn't always the case. For example, in the following sentence, "I want to touch a wall painted green.", we'll need to check the left and right children of the direct object "wall." Also, because "green" is not a direct child of "wall," we'll need to walk the dependency tree to determine that "green" is a modifier of "wall." We'll discuss premodifiers and postmodifiers in more depth in Chapter 6.

The following function examines the chunk and decides what kind of question the chatbot should ask:

```
def determine_question_type(chunk):
❶ question_type = 'yesno'
  for token in chunk:
  ❷ if token.dep_ == 'amod':
    ❸ question_type = 'info'
  return question_type
```

We initialize the question_type variable to a value of yesno, which represents the yes/no question type ❶. Then, in the submitted chunk, we search for a token tagged amod, which stands for adjectival modifier ❷. If we find it, we set the question_type variable to 'info', which represents the information question type ❸.

Once we've determined what question type to use, the following function generates a question from the submitted sentence:

```
def generate_question(doc, question_type):
  sent = ''
  for i,token in enumerate(doc):
    if token.tag_ == 'PRP' and doc[i+1].tag_ == 'VBP':
      sent = 'do ' + doc[i].text
      sent = sent + ' ' + doc[i+1:].text
      break
  doc=nlp(sent)
  for i,token in enumerate(doc):
    if token.tag_ == 'PRP' and token.text == 'I':
      sent = doc[:i].text + ' you ' + doc[i+1:].text
      break
```

```
    doc=nlp(sent)
❶ if question_type == 'info':
      for i,token in enumerate(doc):
        if token.dep_ == 'dobj':
          sent = 'why ' + doc[:i].text + ' one ' +  doc[i+1:].text
          break
❷ if question_type == 'yesno':
      for i,token in enumerate(doc):
        if token.dep_ == 'dobj':
          ❸ sent = doc[:i-1].text + ' a red ' +  doc[i:].text
          break
    doc=nlp(sent)
    sent = doc[0].text.capitalize() +' ' + doc[1:len(doc)-1].text + '?'
    return sent
```

In a sequence of for loops, we convert the submitted statement into a question by performing inversion and changing the personal pronouns. In this example, because there is no modal auxiliary verb in the statement, we add the verb "do" before the personal pronoun to form the question. (Remember that this will only work with certain sentences; in a more complete implementation, we'd have to programmatically figure out which processing approach to take.)

If question_type is set to info, we add the word "why" to the beginning of the question ❶. If the question_type variable is set to yesno ❷, we insert an adjective to modify the direct object in the question. In this example, we've hardcoded the adjective for the sake of simplicity. We've chosen the adjective "red", ❸ which might sound strange in certain sentences. For example, we can say, "Do you want a red orange?" but not "Do you want a red idea?" In a better implementation of this chatbot, we could find a way to programmatically determine a suitable adjective to modify the direct object. We'll come back to that topic in Chapter 6.

Notice also that the algorithm used here assumes that a submitted sentence ends with a punctuation mark, such as "." or "!".

Now that we've defined all the functions, here is the main block of the script:

```
❶ if len(sys.argv) > 1:
    sent = sys.argv[1]
    nlp = spacy.load('en')
❷ doc = nlp(sent)
❸ chunk = find_chunk(doc)
❹ if str(chunk) == '':
    print('The sentence does not contain a direct object.')
    sys.exit()
❺ question_type = determine_question_type(chunk)
❻ question = generate_question(doc, question_type)
  print(question)
else:
  print('You did not submit a sentence!')
```

First, we check whether a user has passed a sentence in as a command line argument ❶. If a sentence has been submitted, we apply spaCy's pipeline to it, creating a Doc object instance ❷.

We then send the doc to the find_chunk function, which should return a noun chunk containing a direct object, such as "a green apple", for further processing ❸. If there is no such noun chunk in the submitted sentence ❹, we'll receive the message "The sentence does not contain a direct object."

Next, we pass the chunk we just extracted to the determine_question_type function, which determines which question to ask based on the chunk's structure ❺.

Finally, we pass the submitted sentence and the type of question to the generate_question function, which will generate an appropriate question and return it as a string ❻.

The script's output depends on the specific sentence submitted. Here are some possible variants:

```
❶ $ python question.py 'I want a green apple.'
  Why do you want a green one?
❷ $ python question.py 'I want an apple.'
  Do you want a red apple?
❸ $ python question.py 'I want...'
  The sentence does not contain a direct object.
❹ $ python question.py
  You did not submit a sentence!
```

If we submit a sentence that contains an adjectival modifier, such as "green" for a direct object like "apple", the script should generate an information question ❶.

If the sentence contains a direct object without an adjectival modifier, the script should respond with a yes/no question ❷.

If we submit a sentence with no direct object, the script should recognize this at once and ask us to resubmit ❸.

Finally, if we forget to submit a sentence, the script should respond with an appropriate message ❹.

Try This

As noted earlier, the script discussed in the preceding section won't work with all sentences. The script adds "do" to form a question, which works only with sentences that contain no auxiliary modal verb.

Enhance the functionality of this script so it can also work with statements containing modal auxiliary verbs. For example, given the following statement, "I might want a green apple," the script should generate "Why might you want a green one?" For details on how to turn a statement containing a modal auxiliary verb into a question, refer to "Turning Statements into Questions" on page 51.

Summary

Linguistic features are at the heart of all NLP tasks. This chapter taught you some techniques for smart text processing and text generation with linguistic features. You learned how to extract phrases of a certain type (say, those that refer to an amount of money), and then wrote a script using dependency labels and part-of-speech tags that generated a meaningful response to the sentence submitted by a user.

We'll return to linguistic features in Chapter 6 where you'll implement them in more complex scenarios.

5

WORKING WITH WORD VECTORS

Word vectors are the series of real numbers that represent the meanings of natural language words. As you learned in Chapter 1, they allow machines to understand human language. In this chapter, you'll use word vectors to calculate the semantic similarity of different texts, which will allow you to, for example, classify those texts based on the topics they cover.

You'll start by taking a conceptual look at word vectors so you can get an idea of how to mathematically calculate the semantic similarity between the words represented in the form of vectors. Then you'll learn how machine learning algorithms generate the word vectors implemented in spaCy models. You'll use spaCy's *similarity method*, which compares the word vectors of container objects to determine the closeness of their meanings. You'll also learn how to use word vectors in practice and perform preprocessing steps, such as choosing keywords, to make your operations more efficient.

Understanding Word Vectors

When building statistical models, we map words to vectors of real numbers that reflect the words' semantic similarity. You can imagine a word vector space as a cloud in which the vectors of words with similar meanings are located nearby. For instance, the vector representing the word "potato" should be closer to the vector of the word "carrot" than to that of the word "crying." To generate these vectors, we must be able to encode the meaning of these words. There are a few approaches to encoding meaning, which we'll outline in this section.

Defining Meaning with Coordinates

One way to generate meaningful word vectors is by assigning an object or category from the real world to each coordinate of a word vector. For example, suppose you're generating word vectors for the following words: Rome, Italy, Athens, and Greece. The word vectors should mathematically reflect the fact that Rome is the capital of Italy and is related to Italy in a way that Athens is not. At the same time, they should reflect the fact that Athens and Rome are capital cities, and that Greece and Italy are countries. Table 5-1 illustrates what this vector space might look like in the form of a matrix.

Table 5-1: A Simplified Word Vector Space

	Country	Capital	Greek	Italian
Italy	1	0	0	1
Rome	0	1	0	1
Greece	1	0	1	0
Athens	0	1	1	0

We've distributed the meaning of each word between its coordinates in a four-dimensional space, representing the categories "Country," "Capital," "Greek," and "Italian." In this simplified example, a coordinate value can be either 1 or 0, indicating whether or not a corresponding word belongs to the category.

Once you have a vector space in which vectors of numbers capture the meaning of corresponding words, you can use vector arithmetic on this vector space to gain insight into a word's meaning. To find out which country Athens is the capital of, you could use the following equation, where each token stands for its corresponding vector and X is an unknown vector:

```
Italy - Rome = X - Athens
```

This equation expresses an analogy in which X represents the word vector that has the same relationship to Athens as Italy has to Rome. To solve for X, we can rewrite the equation like this:

```
X = Italy - Rome + Athens
```

We first subtract the vector Rome from the vector Italy by subtracting the corresponding vector elements. Then we add the sum of the resulting vector and the vector Athens. Table 5-2 summarizes this calculation.

Table 5-2: Performing a Vector Math Operation on a Word Vector Space

		Country	Capital	Greek	Italian
−	Italy	1	0	0	1
	Rome	0	1	0	1
+	Athens	0	1	1	0
	Greece	1	0	1	0

By subtracting the word vector for Rome from the word vector for Italy and then adding the word vector for Athens, we get a vector that is equal to the vector Greece.

Using Dimensions to Represent Meaning

Although the vector space we just created had only four categories, a real-world vector space might require tens of thousands. A vector space of this size would be impractical for most applications, because it would require a huge word-embedding matrix. For example, if you had 10,000 categories and 1,000,000 entities to encode, you'd need a 10,000 × 1,000,000 embedding matrix, making operations on it too time-consuming. The obvious approach to reducing the size of the embedding matrix is to reduce the number of categories in the vector space.

Instead of using coordinates to represent all categories, a real-world implementation of a word vector space uses the distance between vectors to quantify and categorize semantic similarities. The individual dimensions typically don't have inherent meanings. Instead, they represent locations in the vector space, and the distance between vectors indicates the similarity of the corresponding words' meanings.

The following is a fragment of the 300-dimensional word vector space extracted from the *fastText,* a word vector library, which you can download at *https://fasttext.cc/docs/en/english-vectors.html*:

```
compete    -0.0535 -0.0207 0.0574 0.0562 ... -0.0389 -0.0389
equations  -0.0337 0.2013 -0.1587 0.1499 ...  0.1504 0.1151
Upper      -0.1132 -0.0927 0.1991 -0.0302 ... -0.1209 0.2132
mentor      0.0397 0.1639 0.1005 -0.1420 ... -0.2076 -0.0238
reviewer   -0.0424 -0.0304 -0.0031 0.0874 ...  0.1403 -0.0258
```

Each line contains a word represented as a vector of real numbers in multidimensional space. Graphically, we can represent a 300-dimensional vector space like this one with either a 2D or 3D projection. To prepare such a projection, we can use first two or three principal coordinates of a vector, respectively. Figure 5-1 shows vectors from a 300-dimensional vector space in a 2D projection.

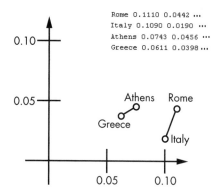

Figure 5-1: A fragment of a 2D projection of a multidimensional vector space

One interesting detail you might notice here is that the lines connecting Greece with Athens and Italy with Rome, respectively, are almost parallel. Their lengths also look comparable. In practice, this means that if you have three out of the above four vectors, you can calculate an approximate location of the missing one, since you know where to shift the vector and how far.

The vectors in the diagram illustrate a country-capital relation, but they could easily have another type of relation, such as male-female, verb tense, and so on.

The Similarity Method

In spaCy, every type of container object has a *similarity method* that allows you to calculate a semantic similarity estimate between two container objects of any type by comparing their word vectors. To calculate the similarity of spans and documents, which don't have their own word vectors, spaCy averages the word vectors of the tokens they contain.

NOTE   *spaCy's small models (those whose model size indicator is sm) don't include word vectors. You can still use the similarity method with these models to compare tokens, spans, and documents, but the results won't be as accurate.*

You can calculate the semantic similarity of two container objects even if the two objects are different. For example, you can compare a Token object with a Span object, a Span object with a Doc object, and so on.

The following example computes how similar a Span object is to a Doc object:

```
>>> doc=nlp('I want a green apple.')
>>> doc.similarity(doc[2:5])
0.7305813588233471
```

This code calculates a semantic similarity estimate between the sentence "I want a green apple." and the phrase "a green apple" derived from this same sentence. As you can see, the computed degree of similarity is high enough to consider the content of two objects similar (the degree of similarity ranges from 0 to 1).

Not surprisingly, the similarity() method returns 1 when you compare an object with itself:

```
>>> doc.similarity(doc)
1.0
>>> doc[2:5].similarity(doc[2:5])
1.0
```

You can also compare a Doc object with a slice from another Doc object:

```
>>> doc2=nlp('I like red oranges.')
>>> doc2.similarity(doc[2:5])
0.28546574467463354
```

Here, we compare the sentence "I like red oranges." stored in doc2 with the span "a green apple" extracted from doc. In this case, the degree of similarity is not so high this time. Yes, oranges and apples are both fruits (the similarity method recognizes this fact), but the verbs "want" and "like" express different states of being.

You can also compare two tokens. In the following example, we compare the Token object "oranges" to a Span object containing a single token "apple."

```
>>> token = doc2[3:4][0]
>>> token
oranges
>>> token.similarity(doc[4:5])
0.3707084280155993
```

First, we explicitly convert the Span object containing a single token "oranges" to a Token object by referring to the first element in the span. Then we calculate how similar it is to the span "apple."

The similarity() method can recognize words that belong to the same or similar categories and that often appear in related contexts, showing a high level of similarity for such words.

Choosing Keywords for Semantic Similarity Calculations

The similarity method will calculate semantic similarity for you, but for the results of that calculation to be useful, you need to choose the right keywords to compare. To understand why, consider the following text snippet:

```
Redwoods are the tallest trees in the world. They are most common in the
coastal forests of California.
```

We might classify this text in a variety of ways depending on the set of categories we want to use. If, for example, we're searching for texts about highest plants on the planet, the phrases "tallest trees" and "in the world" will be the key ones. Comparing these phrases with the search phrases "highest plants" and "on the planet" should show a high level of the semantic similarity. We can do this by extracting noun chunks using a Doc object's doc.noun_chunk property and then checking the similarity of those noun chunks and the search phrases using the similarity method.

But if we're looking for texts about places in the world, "California" will be the keyword. Of course, we don't know in advance which geopolitical name might occur in a text: it could be California or, say, Amazonia. But whatever it is, it should be semantically similar to a word like "geography," which we can compare with the text's other nouns (or, even better, with its named entities only). If we're able to determine that there's a high level of similarity, we can assume that the named entity in question represents a geopolitical name. (We might also extract the token.ent_type attribute of a Token object to do this, as described in Chapter 2. But we wouldn't be able to use named entity recognition to check the similarity of words that aren't named entities, say, fruits.)

Installing Word Vectors

If a spaCy model is installed in your Python environment, you can start using word vectors right away. You can also install a third-party word vector package. Various statistical models use different word vectors, so the results of your operations will differ slightly based on the model you're using. You can try several models to determine which one works better in your particular application.

Taking Advantage of Word Vectors That Come with spaCy Models

Word vectors come as part of many spaCy models. For example, en_vectors _web_lg includes more than one million unique word vectors defined on a 300-dimensional vector space. Check out *https://github.com/explosion/spacy -models/releases/* for details on a particular model.

Typically, small models (those whose names end with sm) don't contain word vectors. Instead, they come with context-sensitive *tensors*, which still allow you to work with the similarity methods to compare tokens, spans, and documents—although at the expense of accuracy.

To follow along with the examples given in this chapter, you can use any spaCy model, even small ones. But you'll get more accurate results if you install a larger model. For details on how to install a spaCy model, refer to "Installing Statistical Models for spaCy" on page 16. Note that you might have more than one model installed in your environment.

Using Third-Party Word Vectors

You can also use third-party packages of word vectors with spaCy. You can check whether a third-party will work better for your application than native word vectors available in a spaCy model. For example, you can use a fastText pretrained model with English word vectors, which you can download at *https://fasttext.cc/docs/en/english-vectors.html*. The name of a package will identify the size of the package and word vectors, and the kind of data used to train the word vectors. For example, *wiki-news-300d-1M.vec.zip* indicates that it contains one million 300-dimensional word vectors trained on Wikipedia and the *statmt.org* news dataset.

After downloading a package, unzip it, and then create a new model from the vectors in the package that you can use with spaCy. To do this, navigate to the folder where you saved the package, and then use the init-model command line utility, like this:

```
$ python -m spacy init-model en /tmp/en_vectors_wiki_lg --vectors-loc wiki-news-300d-1M.vec
```

The command converts the vectors taken from the *wiki-news-300d-1M .vec* file into spaCy's format and creates the new model directory */tmp/en _vectors_wiki_lg* for them. If everything goes well, you'll see the following messages:

```
Reading vectors from wiki-news-300d-1M.vec
Open loc
999994it [02:05, 7968.84it/s]
Creating model...
0it [00:00, ?it/s]

    Successfully compiled vocab
    999731 entries, 999994 vectors
```

Once you've created the model, you can load it like a regular spaCy model:

```
nlp = spacy.load('/tmp/en_vectors_wiki_lg')
```

Then you can create a Doc object as you normally would:

```
doc = nlp(u'Hi there!')
```

Unlike a regular spaCy model, a third-party model converted for use in spaCy might not support some of spaCy's operations against text contained in a doc object. For example, if you try to shred a doc into sentences using doc.sents, you'll get the following error: ValueError: [E030] Sentence boundaries unset...

Comparing spaCy Objects

Let's use word vectors to calculate the similarity of container objects, the most common task for which we use word vectors. In the rest of this chapter, we'll explore some scenarios in which you'd want to determine the semantic similarity of linguistic units.

Using Semantic Similarity for Categorization Tasks

Determining two objects' syntactic similarity can help you sort texts into categories or pick out only the relevant texts. For example, suppose you're sorting through user comments posted to a website to find all the comments related to the word "fruits." Let's say you have the following utterances to evaluate:

```
I want to buy this beautiful book at the end of the week.
Sales of citrus have increased over the last year.
How much do you know about this type of tree?
```

You can easily recognize that only the second sentence is directly related to fruits because it contains the word "citrus." But to pick out this sentence programmatically, you'll have to compare the word vector for the word "fruits" with word vectors in the sample sentences.

Let's start with the simplest but least successful way of doing this task: comparing "fruits" to each of the sentences. As stated earlier, spaCy determines the similarity of two container objects by comparing their corresponding word vectors. To compare a single token with an entire sentence, spaCy averages the sentence's word vectors to generate an entirely new vector. The following script compares each of the preceding sentence samples with the word "fruits":

```
import spacy
nlp = spacy.load('en')
❶ token = nlp(u'fruits')[0]
❷ doc = nlp(u'I want to buy this beautiful book at the end of the week. Sales of
  citrus have increased over the last year. How much do you know about this type
  of tree?')
❸ for sent in doc.sents:
      print(sent.text)
❹     print('similarity to', token.text, 'is', token.similarity(sent),'\n')
```

We first create a Token object for the word "fruits" ❶. Then we apply the pipeline to the sentences we're categorizing, creating a single Doc object to hold all of them ❷. We shred the doc into sentences ❸, and then print each of the sentences and their semantic similarity to the token "fruits," which we acquire using the token object's similarity method ❹.

The output should look something like this (although the actual figures will depend on the model you use):

```
I want to buy this beautiful book at the end of the week.
similarity to fruits is 0.06307832979619851
Sales of citrus have increased over the last year.
similarity to fruits is 0.2712141843864381
How much do you know about this type of tree?
similarity to fruits is 0.24646341651210604
```

The degree of similarity between the word "fruits" and the first sentence is very small, indicating that the sentence has nothing to do with fruits. The second sentence—the one that includes the word "citrus"—is the most closely related to "fruits," meaning the script correctly identified the relevant sentence.

But notice that the script also identified the third sentence as being somehow related to fruits, probably because it includes the word "tree," and fruits grow on trees. It would be naive to think that the similarity measuring algorithm "knows" that orange and citrus are fruits. All it knows is that these words ("orange" and "citrus") often share the same context with word "fruit" and therefore they've been put close to it in the vector space. But the word "tree" can also often be found in the same context as the word "fruit." For example, the phrase "fruit tree" is not uncommon. For that reason the level of similarity calculated between "fruits" (or "fruit" as its lemma) and "tree" is close to the result we got for "citrus" and "fruits."

There's another problem with this approach to categorizing texts. In practice, of course, you might sometimes have to deal with texts that are much larger than the sample texts used in this section. If the text you're averaging is very large, the most important words might have little to no effect on the syntactic similarity value.

To get more accurate results from the similarity method, we'll need to perform some preparations on a text. Let's look at how we can improve the script.

Extracting Nouns as a Preprocessing Step

A better technique for performing categorization would be to extract the most important words and compare only those. Preparing a text for processing in this way is called *preprocessing*, and it can help make your NLP operations more successful. For example, instead of comparing the word vectors for the entire objects, you could try comparing the word vectors for certain parts of speech. In most cases, you'll focus on nouns—whether they act as subjects, direct objects, or indirect objects—to recognize the meaning conveyed in the text in which they occur. For example, in the sentence "Nearly all wild lions live in Africa," you'll probably focus on lions, Africa, or lions in Africa. Similarly, in the sentence about fruits, we focused on picking out the noun "citrus." In other cases, you'll need other words, like verbs, to decide what a text is about. Suppose you run an agricultural produce business and must classify offers from those who produce, process, and sell farm products. You often see sentences like, "We grow vegetables," or "We take tomatoes for processing." In this example, the verbs are just as important as nouns in the utterances in the previous examples.

Let's modify the script on page 70. Instead of comparing "fruits" to entire sentences, we'll compare it to the sentences' nouns only:

```
import spacy
nlp = spacy.load('en')
❶ token = nlp(u'fruits')[0]
doc = nlp(u'I want to buy this beautiful book at the end of the week. Sales of
citrus have increased over the last year. How much do you know about this type
of tree?')
```

```
  similarity = {}
❷ for i, sent in enumerate(doc.sents):
  ❸ noun_span_list = [sent[j].text for j in range(len(sent)) if sent[j].pos_
     == 'NOUN']
  ❹ noun_span_str = ' '.join(noun_span_list)
  ❺ noun_span_doc = nlp(noun_span_str)
  ❻ similarity.update({i:token.similarity(noun_span_doc)})
  print(similarity)
```

We start by defining the token "fruits," which is then used for a series of comparisons ❶. Iterating over the tokens in each sentence ❷, we extract the nouns and store them in a Python list ❸. Next, we join the nouns in the list into a plain string ❹, and then convert that string into a Doc object ❺. We then compare this Doc with the token "fruits" to determine their degree of semantic similarity. We store each token's syntactic similarity value in a Python dictionary ❻, which we finally print out.

The script's output should look something like this:

```
{0: 0.17012682516221458, 1: 0.5063824302533686, 2: 0.6277196645922878}
```

If you compare these figures with the results of the previous script, you'll notice that this time the level of the similarity with the word "fruits" is higher for each sentence. But the overall results look similar: the similarity of the first sentence is the lowest, whereas the similarity of the other two are much higher.

Try This

In the previous example, comparing "fruits" to nouns only, you improved the results of the similarity calculations by taking into account only the words that matter most (nouns, in this case). You compared the word "fruits" with all the nouns extracted from each sentence, combined. Taking it one step further, you could look at how each of these nouns is semantically related to the word "fruits" to find out which one shows the highest level of similarity. This can be useful in evaluating the overall similarity of the document to the word "fruits." To accomplish this, you need to modify the previous script so it determines the similarity between the token "fruits" and each of the nouns in a sentence, finding the noun that shows the highest level of similarity.

Extracting and Comparing Named Entities

In some cases, instead of extracting every noun from the texts you're comparing, you might want to extract a certain kind of noun only, such as named entities. Let's say you're comparing the following texts:

"Google Search, often referred to as simply Google, is the most used search engine nowadays. It handles a huge number of searches each day."

"Microsoft Windows is a family of proprietary operating systems developed and sold by Microsoft. The company also produces a wide range of other software for desktops and servers."

"Titicaca is a large, deep, mountain lake in the Andes. It is known as the highest navigable lake in the world."

Ideally, your script should recognize that the first two texts are about large technology companies, but the third text isn't. But comparing all the nouns in this text wouldn't be very helpful, because many of them, such as "number" in the first sentence, aren't relevant to the context. The differences between the sentences involve the following words: "Google," "Search," "Microsoft," "Windows," "Titicaca," and "Andes." spaCy recognizes all of these as named entities, which makes it a breeze to find and extract them from a text, as illustrated in the following script:

```
import spacy
nlp = spacy.load('en')
#first sample text
doc1 = nlp(u'Google Search, often referred to as simply Google, is the most
used search engine nowadays. It handles a huge number of searches each day.')
#second sample text
doc2 = nlp(u'Microsoft Windows is a family of proprietary operating systems
developed and sold by Microsoft. The company also produces a wide range of
other software for desktops and servers.')
#third sample text
doc3 = nlp(u"Titicaca is a large, deep, mountain lake in the Andes. It is
known as the highest navigable lake in the world.")
❶ docs = [doc1,doc2,doc3]
❷ spans = {}
❸ for j,doc in enumerate(docs):
❹     named_entity_span = [doc[i].text for i in range(len(doc)) if
          doc[i].ent_type != 0]
❺     print(named_entity_span)
❻     named_entity_span = ' '.join(named_entity_span)
❼     named_entity_span = nlp(named_entity_span)
❽     spans.update({j:named_entity_span})
```

We group the Docs with the sample texts into a list to make it possible to iterate over them in a loop ❶. We define a Python dictionary to store the keywords for each text ❷. In a loop iterating over the Docs ❸, we extract these keywords in a separate list for each text, selecting only the words marked as named entities ❹. Then we print out the list to see what it contains ❺. Next, we convert this list into a plain string ❻ to which we then apply the pipeline, converting it to a Doc object ❼. We then append the Doc to the spans dictionary defined earlier ❽.

The script should produce the following output:

```
['Google', 'Search', 'Google']
['Microsoft', 'Windows', 'Microsoft']
['Titicaca', 'Andes']
```

Now we can see the words in each text whose vectors we'll compare.

Next, we call `similarity()` on these spans and print the results:

```
print('doc1 is similar to doc2:',spans[0].similarity(spans[1]))
print('doc1 is similar to doc3:',spans[0].similarity(spans[2]))
print('doc2 is similar to doc3:',spans[1].similarity(spans[2]))
```

This time the output should look as follows:

```
doc1 is similar to doc2: 0.7864886939527678
doc1 is similar to doc3: 0.6797676349647936
doc2 is similar to doc3: 0.6621659567003596
```

These figures indicate that the highest level of similarity exists between the first and second texts, which are both about American IT companies. How can word vectors "know" about this fact? They probably know because the words "Google" and "Microsoft" have been found more often in the same texts of the training text corpus rather than in the company of the words "Titicaca" and "Andes."

Summary

In this chapter, you worked with word vectors, which are vectors of real numbers that represent the meanings of words. These representations let you use math to determine the semantic similarity of linguistic units, a useful task for categorizing texts.

But the math approach might not work as well when you're trying to determine the similarity of two texts without applying any preliminary steps to those texts. By applying preprocessing, you can reduce the text to the words that are most important in figuring out what the text is about. In particularly large texts, you might pick out the named entities found in it, because they most likely best describe the text's category.

6

FINDING PATTERNS AND WALKING DEPENDENCY TREES

If you want your application to categorize a text, extract specific phrases from it, or determine how semantically similar it is to another text, it must be able to "understand" an utterance submitted by a user and generate a meaningful response to it.

You've already learned some techniques for performing these tasks. This chapter discusses two more approaches: using word sequence patterns to classify and generate text, and walking the syntactic dependency tree of an utterance to extract necessary pieces of information from it. I'll introduce you to spaCy's Matcher tool to find patterns. I'll also discuss when you might still need to rely on context to determine the proper processing approach.

Word Sequence Patterns

A *word sequence pattern* consists of features of words that impose a certain requirement on each word in the sequence. For example, the phrase "I can" will match the following word sequence pattern: "pronoun + modal auxiliary verb." By searching for word sequence patterns, you can recognize word sequences with similar linguistic features, making it possible to categorize input and handle it properly.

For example, when you receive a question that begins with a word sequence that uses the pattern "modal auxiliary verb + proper noun," such as "Can George," you know that this question is about the ability, possibility, permission, or obligation of someone or something that the proper noun refers to.

In the following sections, you'll learn to classify sentences by identifying common patterns of linguistic features.

Finding Patterns Based on Linguistic Features

We need to find patterns in texts because, in most cases, we won't be able to find even two identical sentences within a text. Typically, a text is composed of different sentences, each of which contains different words. It would be impractical to write the code to process each sentence in a text.

Fortunately, some sentences that look completely different might follow the same word sequence patterns. For example, consider the following two sentences: "We can overtake them." and "You must specify it.". These sentences have no words in common. But if you look at the syntactic dependency labels assigned to the words in the sentences, a pattern emerges, as shown in the following script:

```
import spacy
nlp = spacy.load('en')
doc1 = nlp(u'We can overtake them.')
doc2 = nlp(u'You must specify it.')
❶ for i in range(len(doc1)-1):
❷   if doc1[i].dep_ == doc2[i].dep_:
❸     print(doc1[i].text, doc2[i].text, doc1[i].dep_, spacy.explain(doc1[i].dep_))
```

Because both sentences have the same number of words, we can iterate over the words in both sentences within a single loop ❶. If the dependency label is the same for the words that have the same index in both sentences ❷, we print these words along with the label assigned to them, as well as a description for each label ❸.

The output should look as follows:

```
We       You     nsubj  nominal subject
can      must    aux    auxiliary
overtake specify ROOT   None
them     it      dobj   direct object
```

As you can see, the list of dependency labels is identical for both sentences. This means that these sentences follow the same word sequence pattern based on the following syntactic dependency labels: "subject + auxiliary + verb + direct object."

Also notice that the list of part-of-speech tags (coarse-grained and fined-grained) is also identical for these sample sentences. If we replace all references to .dep_ with .pos_ in the previous script, we'll get the following results:

```
We        You     PRON  pronoun
can       must    VERB  verb
overtake  specify VERB  verb
them      it      PRON  pronoun
```

The sample sentences match not only the syntactic dependency label pattern, but also the pattern of part-of-speech tags.

Try This

In the previous example, we created two Doc objects—one for each sample sentence. But in practice, a text usually consists of numerous sentences, which makes a Doc-per-sentence approach impractical. Rewrite the script so it creates a single Doc object. Then use the doc.sents property introduced in Chapter 2 to operate on each sentence.

But note that doc.sents is a generator object, which means it's not subscriptable—you can't refer to its items by index. To solve this issue, convert the doc.sents to a list, as follows:

```
sents = list(doc.sents)
```

And, of course, you can iterate over a doc.sents in a for loop to obtain the sents in order, as they're requested by the loop.

Checking an Utterance for a Pattern

In the preceding example, we compared two sample sentences to find a pattern based on their shared linguistic features. But in practice, we'll rarely want to compare sentences to one another to determine whether they share a common pattern. Instead, it'll be more useful to check a submitted sentence against the pattern we're already interested in.

For example, let's say we were trying to find utterances in user input that express one of the following: ability, possibility, permission, or obligation (as opposed to utterances that describe real actions that have occurred, are occurring, or occur regularly). For instance, we want to find "I can do it." but not "I've done it."

To distinguish between utterances, we might check whether an utterance satisfies the following pattern: "subject + auxiliary + verb + . . . + direct object . . .". The ellipses indicate that the direct object isn't necessarily located immediately behind the verb, making this pattern a little different from the one in the preceding example.

The following sentence satisfies the pattern: "I might send them a card as a reminder.". In this sentence, the noun "card" is a direct object, and the pronoun "them" is an indirect object that separates it from the verb "send." The pattern doesn't specify a position for the direct object in the sentence; it simply requires its presence.

Figure 6-1 shows a graphical depiction of this design:

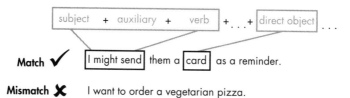

Figure 6-1: Checking submitted utterances against a word sequence pattern based on linguistic features

In the following script, we define a function that implements this pattern, and then test it on a sample sentence:

```
import spacy
nlp = spacy.load('en')
❶ def dep_pattern(doc):
  ❷ for i in range(len(doc)-1):
    ❸ if doc[i].dep_ == 'nsubj' and doc[i+1].dep_ == 'aux' and
       doc[i+2].dep_ == 'ROOT':
      ❹ for tok in doc[i+2].children:
          if tok.dep_ == 'dobj':
            ❺ return True
  ❻ return False
❼ doc = nlp(u'We can overtake them.')
  if ❽dep_pattern(doc):
    print('Found')
  else:
    print('Not found')
```

In this script, we define the dep_pattern function that takes a Doc object as parameter ❶. In the function, we iterate over the Doc object's tokens ❷, searching for a "subject + auxiliary + verb" pattern ❸. If we find this pattern, we check whether the verb has a direct object among its syntactic children ❹. Finally, if we find a direct object, the function returns True ❺. Otherwise, it returns False ❻.

In the main code, we apply the text-processing pipeline to the sample sentence ❼ and send the Doc object to the dep_pattern function ❽, outputting Found if the sample satisfies the pattern implemented in the function or Not found otherwise.

Because the sample used in this example satisfies the pattern, the script should produce the following output:

```
Found
```

You'll see some examples of using the dep_pattern function in some of the following sections.

Using spaCy's Matcher to Find Word Sequence Patterns

In the previous section, you learned how to find a word sequence pattern in a doc by iterating over its tokens and checking their linguistic features. In fact, spaCy has a predefined feature for this task called *Matcher*, a tool that is specially designed to find sequences of tokens based on pattern rules. For example, an implementation of the "subject + auxiliary + verb" pattern with Matcher might look like this:

```
  import spacy
  from spacy.matcher import Matcher
  nlp = spacy.load("en")
❶ matcher = Matcher(nlp.vocab)
❷ pattern = [{"DEP": "nsubj"}, {"DEP": "aux"}, {"DEP": "ROOT"}]
❸ matcher.add("NsubjAuxRoot", None, pattern)
  doc = nlp(u"We can overtake them.")
❹ matches = matcher(doc)
❺ for match_id, start, end in matches:
      span = doc[start:end]
❻     print("Span: ", span.text)
      print("The positions in the doc are: ", start, "-", end)
```

We create a Matcher instance, passing in the vocabulary object shared with the documents the Matcher will work on ❶. Then we define a pattern, specifying the dependency labels that a word sequence should match ❷. We add the newly created pattern to the Matcher ❸.

Next, we can apply the Matcher to a sample text and obtain the matching tokens in a list ❹. Then we iterate over this list ❺, printing out the start and end positions of the pattern tokens in the text ❻.

The script should produce the following output:

```
Span: We can overtake
The positions in the doc are: 0 - 3
```

Matcher allows you to find a pattern in a text without iterating explicitly over the text's tokens, thus hiding implementation details from you. As a result, you can obtain the start and end positions of the words composing a sequence that satisfies the specified pattern. This approach can be very useful when you're interested in a sequence of words that immediately follow one another.

But often you need a pattern that includes words scattered over the sentence. For example, you might need to implement such patterns as the "subject + auxiliary + verb + . . . + direct object . . ." pattern we used in "Checking an Utterance for a Pattern" on page 77. The problem is that you don't know in advance how many words can occur between the "subject + auxiliary + verb" sequence and the direct object. Matcher doesn't allow you to define such patterns. For this reason, I'll define patterns manually for the remainder of this chapter.

Applying Several Patterns

You can apply several matching patterns to an utterance to make sure it satisfies all your conditions. For example, you might check an utterance against two patterns: one that implements a dependency label sequence (as discussed in "Checking an Utterance for a Pattern" on page 77) and one that checks against a sequence of part-of-speech tags. This might be helpful, if, say, you want to make sure that the direct object in an utterance is a personal pronoun. If so, you can start the procedure of determining the noun that gives its meaning to the pronoun and is mentioned elsewhere in the discourse.

Diagrammatically, this design might look like Figure 6-2.

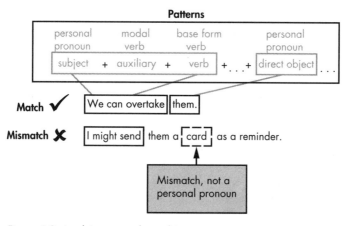

Figure 6-2: Applying several matching patterns to user input

In addition to using the dependency label sequence defined in "Checking an Utterance for a Pattern", you can define a new function by implementing a pattern based on part-of-speech tags. The part-of-speech tag pattern might search the sentence to make sure that the subject and the direct object are personal pronouns. This new function might implement the following pattern: "personal pronoun + modal auxiliary verb + base form verb + . . . + personal pronoun . . .".

Here is the code:

```
import spacy
nlp = spacy.load('en')
#Insert the dep_pattern function from a previous listing here
#...
```

```
❶ def pos_pattern(doc):
 ❷ for token in doc:
        if token.dep_ == 'nsubj' and token.tag_ != 'PRP':
            return False
        if token.dep_ == 'aux' and token.tag_ != 'MD':
            return False
        if token.dep_ == 'ROOT' and token.tag_ != 'VB':
            return False
        if token.dep_ == 'dobj' and token.tag_ != 'PRP':
            return False
 ❸ return True
   #Testing code
   doc = nlp(u'We can overtake them.')
❹ if dep_pattern(doc) and pos_pattern(doc):
       print('Found')
   else:
       print('Not found')
```

We start by adding the code for the dep_pattern function defined in a previous script. To create the second pattern, we define the pos_pattern function ❶, which contains a for loop with a series of if statements in it ❷. Each if statement checks whether a certain part of a sentence matches a certain part-of-speech tag. When the function detects a mismatch, it returns False. Otherwise, after all the checks have occurred and no mismatch has been detected, the function returns True ❸.

To test the patterns, we apply the pipeline to a sentence, and then check whether the sentence matches both patterns ❹. Because the sample used in this example matches both patterns, we should see the following output:

```
Found
```

But if we replace the sample sentence with this one: "I might send them a card as a reminder.", we should see this output:

```
Not found
```

The reason is that the sentence doesn't match the part-of-speech tag pattern, because the direct object "card" isn't a personal pronoun, even though the sentence fully satisfies the conditions of the first pattern.

Creating Patterns Based on Customized Features

When creating a word sequence pattern, you might need to enhance the functionality of the linguistic features spaCy provides by customizing them for your needs. For example, you might want the preceding script to recognize another pattern that distinguishes pronouns according to number (whether they're singular or plural). Once again, this could be useful when you need to find the noun in a previous utterance to which the pronoun refers.

Although spaCy separates nouns by number, it doesn't do this for pronouns. But the ability to recognize whether a pronoun is plural or singular can be very useful in the task of meaning recognition or information extraction. For example, consider the following discourse:

```
The trucks are traveling slowly. We can overtake them.
```

If we can establish that the direct object "them" in the second sentence is a plural pronoun, we'll have reason to believe that it refers to the plural noun "trucks" in the first sentence. We often use this technique to recognize a pronoun's meaning based on the context.

The following script defines a pron_pattern function, which finds any direct object in the submitted sentence, determines whether that direct object is a personal pronoun, and then determines whether the pronoun is singular or plural. The script then applies the function to a sample sentence after testing for the two patterns defined in "Checking an Utterance for a Pattern" on page 77 and "Applying Several Patterns" on page 80.

```
import spacy
nlp = spacy.load('en')
#Insert the dep_pattern and pos_pattern functions from the previous
listings here
#...
❶ def pron_pattern(doc):
❷   plural = ['we','us','they','them']
    for token in doc:
❸     if token.dep_ == 'dobj' and token.tag_ == 'PRP':
❹       if token.text in plural:
❺         return 'plural'
        else:
❻         return 'singular'
❼   return 'not found'
  doc = nlp(u'We can overtake them.')
  if dep_pattern(doc) and pos_pattern(doc):
      print('Found:', 'the pronoun in position of direct object is',
      pron_pattern(doc))
  else:
      print('Not found')
```

We start by adding the dep_pattern and pos_pattern functions defined in "Checking an Utterance for a Pattern" and "Applying Several Patterns" to the script. In the pron_pattern function ❶, we define a Python list that includes all the possible plural personal pronouns ❷. Next, we define a loop that iterates over the tokens in the submitted sentence, looking for a direct object that is a personal pronoun ❸. If we find such a token, we check whether it's in the list of plural personal pronouns ❹. If so, the function returns plural ❺. Otherwise, it returns singular ❻. If the function either failed to detect a direct object or found one that isn't a personal pronoun, it returns Not found ❼.

For the sentence "We can overtake them.", we should get the following output:

```
Found: the pronoun in position of direct object is plural
```

We could use this information to find a corresponding noun for the pronoun in the previous sentence.

Choosing Which Patterns to Apply

Once you define these patterns, you can choose which ones to apply for each situation. Notice that even if a sentence fails to fully satisfy the dep_pattern and pos_pattern functions, it might still match the pron_pattern function. For example, the sentence "I know it." doesn't match either the dep_pattern or pos_pattern functions, because it doesn't have a modal auxiliary verb. But it satisfies pron_pattern because it contains a personal pronoun that is the direct object of the sentence.

This loose coupling between the patterns lets you use them with other patterns or independently. For example, you might use dep_pattern, which checks a sentence against the "subject + auxiliary + verb + . . . + direct object . . ." pattern in conjunction with, say, a "noun + modal auxiliary verb + base form verb + . . . + noun . . ." pattern, if you wanted to be sure that the subject and the direct object in the sentence are nouns. These two patterns would match the following example:

```
Developers might follow this rule.
```

As you might guess, the ability to combine patterns in different ways allows you to handle more scenarios with less code.

Using Word Sequence Patterns in Chatbots to Generate Statements

As stated earlier, the most challenging tasks in NLP are understanding and generating natural language text. A chatbot must understand a user's input and then generate a proper response to it. Word sequence patterns based on linguistic features can help you implement these functions.

In Chapter 4, you learned how to turn a statement into a relevant question to continue a conversation with a user. Using word sequence patterns, you could generate other kinds of responses, too, such as relevant statements.

Suppose your chatbot has received the following user input:

```
The symbols are clearly distinguishable. I can recognize them promptly.
```

The chatbot might react as follows:

```
I can recognize symbols promptly too.
```

You can use the patterns implemented in the previous sections to accomplish this text generation task. The list of steps might look like this:

1. Check the conversational input against the dep_pattern and pos_pattern functions defined previously to find an utterance that follows the "subject + auxiliary + verb + . . . + direct object . . ." and "pronoun + modal auxiliary verb + base form verb + . . . + pronoun . . ." patterns, respectively.

2. Check the utterance found in step 1 against the pron_pattern pattern to determine whether the direct object personal pronoun is plural or singular.

3. Find the noun that gives its meaning to the pronoun by searching for a noun that has the same number as the personal pronoun.

4. Replace the pronoun that acts as the direct object in the sentence located in step 1 with the noun found in step 3.

5. Append the word "too" to the end of the generated utterance.

The following script implements these steps. It uses the dep_pattern, pos_pattern, and pron_pattern functions defined earlier in this chapter (their code is omitted to save space). It also introduces two new functions: find_noun and gen_utterance. For convenience, we'll walk through the code in three steps: the initial operations and the find_noun function, which finds the noun that matches the personal pronoun; the gen_utterance function, which generates a relevant statement from that question; and finally, the code that tests an utterance. Here is the first part:

```
import spacy
nlp = spacy.load('en')
#Insert the dep_pattern, pos_pattern and pron_pattern functions from the
previous listings here
#...
❶ def find_noun(❷sents, ❸num):
    if num == 'plural':
    ❹ taglist = ['NNS','NNPS']
    if num == 'singular':
    ❺ taglist = ['NN','NNP']
  ❻ for sent in reversed(sents):
    ❼ for token in sent:
      ❽ if token.tag_ in taglist:
          return token.text
    return 'Noun not found'
```

After inserting the code of the dep_pattern, pos_pattern, and pron_pattern functions, we define the find_noun function, which takes two parameters ❶. The first one contains a list of the sentences from the beginning of the discourse up to the sentence that satisfies all the patterns here. In this example, this list will include all the sentences from the discourse, because only the last sentence satisfies all the patterns ❷. But the noun that gives its meaning to the pronoun can be found in one of the previous sentences.

The second parameter sent to find_noun is the number of the direct object pronoun in the sentence that satisfies all the patterns ❸. The pron_pattern function determines this. If the value of this argument is 'plural', we define a Python list containing fine-grained part-of-speech tags used in spaCy to mark plural nouns ❹. If it's 'singular', we create a tag list containing fine-grained part-of-speech tags used to mark singular nouns ❺.

In a for loop, we iterate over the sentences in reverse order, starting from the sentence that is the closest to the sentence containing the pronoun to be replaced ❻. We start with the closest sentence, because the noun we're searching for will most likely be there. Here, we use Python's reversed function that returns a reverse iterator over the list. In the inner loop, we iterate over the tokens in each sentence ❼, looking for a token whose fine-grained part-of-speech tag is in the tag list defined earlier ❽.

Then we define the gen_utterance function, which generates our new statement:

```
def gen_utterance(doc, noun):
    sent = ''
❶  for i,token in enumerate(doc):
❷    if token.dep_ == 'dobj' and token.tag_ == 'PRP':
❸      sent = doc[:i].text + ' ' + noun + ' ' + doc[i+1:len(doc)-2].text + 'too.'
❹      return sent
❺  return 'Failed to generate an utterance'
```

We use a for loop to iterate over the tokens in the sentence ❶, looking for a direct object that is a personal pronoun ❷. Once we've found one, we generate a new utterance. We change the original sentence by replacing the personal pronoun with the matching noun and appending "too" to the end of it ❸. The function then returns this newly generated utterance ❹. If we haven't found a direct object in the form of a personal pronoun, the function returns an error message ❺.

Now that we have all the functions in place, we can test them on a sample utterance using the following code:

```
❶ doc = nlp(u'The symbols are clearly distinguishable. I can recognize them
  promptly.')
❷ sents = list(doc.sents)
  response = ''
  noun = ''
❸ for i, sent in enumerate(sents):
    if dep_pattern(sent) and pos_pattern(sent):
❹    noun = find_noun(sents[:i], pron_pattern(sent))
      if noun != 'Noun not found':
❺      response = gen_utterance(sents[i],noun)
      break
  print(response)
```

After applying the pipeline to the sample discourse ❶, we convert it to the list of sentences ❷. Then we iterate over this list ❸, searching for the sentence that matches the patterns defined in the dep_pattern and pos_pattern functions. Next, we determine the noun that gives the meaning to the pronoun in the sentence found in the previous step, using the find_noun function ❹. Finally, we call the get_utterance function to generate a response utterance ❺.

The output of the preceding code should look like this:

```
I can recognize symbols too.
```

Try This

Notice that there's still room for improvement in the preceding code, because the original statement included the article "the" in front of the noun "symbols." A better output would include the same article in front of the noun. To generate a statement that makes the most sense in this context, expand on the script so that it inserts the article "the" in front of the noun, making it "I can recognize the symbols too." For that, you'll need to check whether the noun is preceded by an article, and then add that article.

Extracting Keywords from Syntactic Dependency Trees

Finding a sequence of words in an utterance that satisfies a certain pattern allows you to construct a grammatically correct response—either a statement or a question, based on the submitted text. But these patterns aren't always useful for extracting the meaning of texts.

For example, in the ticket-booking application in Chapter 2, a user might submit a sentence like this:

```
I need an air ticket to Berlin.
```

You could easily find the user's intended destination by searching for the pattern "to + GPE" where GPE is a named entity for countries, cities, and states. This pattern would match phrases like "to London," "to California," and so on.

But suppose the user submitted one of the following utterances instead:

```
I am going to the conference in Berlin. I need an air ticket.
I am going to the conference, which will be held in Berlin. I would like to
book an air ticket.
```

As you can see, the "to + GPE" pattern wouldn't find the destination in either example. In both cases, "to" directly refers to "the conference," not to Berlin. You'd need something like "to + . . . + GPE" instead. But how would you know what's required—or what's allowed—between "to" and "GPE"? For example, the following sentence contains the "to + . . . + GPE" pattern but has nothing to do with booking a ticket to Berlin:

```
I want to book a ticket on a direct flight without landing in Berlin.
```

Often, you need to examine relations between the words in a sentence to obtain necessary pieces of information. This is where walking the dependency tree of the sentence could help a lot.

Walking a dependency tree means navigating through it in custom order—not necessarily from the first token to the last one. For example, you can stop iterating a dependency tree just after the required component is found. Remember that a sentence's dependency tree shows the syntactic relationships between pairs of words. We often represent these as arrows connecting the head with the child of a relation. Every word in a sentence is involved in at least one of the relations. This guarantees that you'll pass through each word in a sentence when walking through the entire dependency tree generated for that sentence if you start from ROOT.

In this section, we'll examine a sentence's structure to figure out a user's intended meaning.

Walking a Dependency Tree for Information Extraction

Let's return to the ticket-booking application example. To find a user's intended destination, you might need to iterate over the dependency tree of a sentence to determine whether "to" is semantically related to "Berlin." This is easy to accomplish if you remember the head/child syntactic relations that compose a dependency tree, which was introduced in the "Head and Child" box on page 25.

Figure 6-3 shows the dependency tree for the sentence, "I am going to the conference in Berlin":

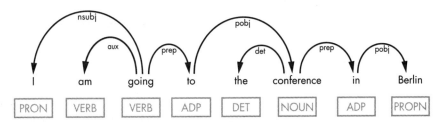

Figure 6-3: A syntactic dependency tree of an utterance

The verb "going" is the root of the sentence, meaning it's not a child of any other word. Its child to the immediate right is "to." If you walk through the dependency tree, moving to the child to the immediate right of each word, you'll finally reach "Berlin." This shows that there's a semantic connection between "to" and "Berlin" in this sentence.

Iterating over the Heads of Tokens

Now let's figure out how to express the relation between "to" and "Berlin" in the sentence programmatically. One way is to walk the dependency tree from left to right, starting from "to," choosing only the immediate right child of each word along the way. If you can go from "to" to "Berlin" this way, you can reasonably assume that there's a semantic connection between the two words.

But this approach has a drawback. In some cases, a word might have more than one right child. For example, in the sentence "I am going to the conference on spaCy, which will be held in Berlin," the word "conference" has two immediate right children: the words "on" and "held." This forces you to check multiple branches, complicating the code.

On the other hand, although a head can have multiple children, each word in a sentence has exactly one head. This means you can instead move from right to left, starting from "Berlin" and trying to reach "to." The following script implements this process in the det_destination function:

```
import spacy
nlp = spacy.load('en')
#Here's the function that figures out the destination
❶ def det_destination(doc):
    for i, token in enumerate(doc):
❷     if token.ent_type != 0 and token.ent_type_ == 'GPE':
❸       while True:
❹         token = token.head
          if token.text == 'to':
❺           return doc[i].text
❻         if token.head == token:
            return 'Failed to determine'
    return 'Failed to determine'
#Testing the det_destination function
doc = nlp(u'I am going to the conference in Berlin.')
❼ dest = det_destination(doc)
print('It seems the user wants a ticket to ' + dest)
```

In the det_destination function ❶, we iterate over the tokens in the submitted utterance, looking for a GPE entity ❷. If it's found, we start a while loop ❸ that iterates over the head of each token, starting from the token containing the GPE entity ❹. The loop stops when it reaches either the token containing "to" ❺ or the root of the sentence. We can check for the root by comparing a token to its head ❻, because the head of the root token always refers to itself. (Alternatively, we can check for the ROOT tag.)

To test this function, we apply the pipeline to the sample sentence and then invoke the det_destination function on it ❼.

The script should generate the following output:

```
It seems the user wants a ticket to Berlin
```

If we change the sample sentence so it doesn't contain "to" or a GPE named entity, we should get the following output:

```
It seems the user wants a ticket to Failed to determine
```

We can improve the script so it uses another message for cases when it fails to determine the user's destination.

Condensing a Text Using Dependency Trees

The syntactic dependency tree approach isn't limited to chatbots, of course. You could use it, for example, in report-processing applications. Say, you need to develop an application that has to condense retail reports by extracting only the most important information from them.

For example, you might want to select the sentences containing numbers, producing a concise summary of the data on sales volume, revenue, and costs. (You learned how to extract numbers in Chapter 4.) Then, to make your new report more concise, you might shorten the selected sentences.

As a quick example, consider the following sentence:

The product sales hit a new record in the first quarter, with 18.6 million units sold.

After processing, it should look like this:

The product sales hit 18.6 million units sold.

To accomplish this, you can analyze the dependency trees of sentences by following these steps:

1. Extract the entire phrase containing the number (it's 18.6 in this example) by walking the heads of tokens, starting from the token containing the number and moving from left to right.

2. Walk the dependency tree from the main word of the extracted phrase (the one whose head is out of the phrase) to the main verb of the sentence, iterating over the heads and picking them up to be used in a new sentence.

3. Pick up the main verb's subject, along with its leftward children, which typically include a determiner and possibly some other modifiers.

Figure 6-4 represents this process.

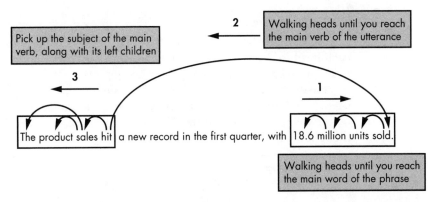

Figure 6-4: An example of condensing a sentence to include only important elements

Let's start with the first step, which in this example should extract the phrase "18.6 million units sold.". The following code snippet illustrates how to do this programmatically:

```
doc = nlp(u"The product sales hit a new record in the first quarter, with 18.6
million units sold.")
phrase = ''
for token in doc:
❶ if token.pos_ == 'NUM':
        while True:
            phrase = phrase + ' ' + token.text
        ❷ token = token.head
        ❸ if token not in list(token.head.lefts):
                phrase = phrase + ' ' + token.text
            ❹ break
    ❺ break
print(phrase.strip())
```

We iterate over the sentence's tokens, looking for one that represents a number ❶. If we find one, we start a while loop that iterates over right-hand heads ❷, starting from the number token and then appending the text of each head to the phrase variable to form a new phrase. To make sure the head of the next token is to the right of that token, we check whether the token is in the list of its head's left children ❸. Once this condition returns false, we break from the while loop ❹ and then from the outer for loop ❺.

Next, we walk the heads of tokens, starting from the main word of the phrase containing the number ("sold" in this example) until we reach the main verb of the sentence ("hit" in this example), excluding the adposition ("with" in this example). We can implement this as shown in the following listing:

```
while True:
❶ token = doc[token.i].head
  if token.pos_ != 'ADP':
  ❷ phrase = token.text + phrase
❸ if token.dep_ == 'ROOT':
❹ break
```

We walk the heads of tokens ❶ in a while loop, appending the text of each head to the phrase being formed ❷. After reaching the main verb (marked as ROOT) ❸, we break from the loop ❹.

Finally, we pick up the subject of the sentence, along with its left children: "The" and "product." In this example, the subject is "sales," so we pick up the following noun chunk: "The product sales." This can be done with the following code:

```
❶ for tok in token.lefts:
  ❷ if tok.dep_ == 'nsubj':
```

```
❸   phrase = ' '.join([tok.text for tok in tok.lefts]) + ' ' + tok.text + ' '
    + phrase
    break
❹ print(phrase)
```

We start by iterating over the main verb's children ❶, searching for the subject ❷. Then we prepend the subject's children and the subject of the phrase ❸. To see the resulting phrase, we print it ❹.

The output should look like this:

```
The product sales hit 18.6 million units sold.
```

The result is a condensed version of the original sentence.

Try This

Write a script that condenses financial reports by extracting only those sentences that contain phrases referring to an amount of money. Also, the script needs to condense the selected sentences so they include only the subject, the main verb, the phrase referring to an amount of money, and the tokens you can pick up when walking the heads starting from the main word of the money phrase up to the main verb of the sentence. For example, given the following sentence:

```
The company, whose profits reached a record high this year, largely attributed
to changes in management, earned a total revenue of $4.26 million.
```

Your script should return this sentence:

```
The company earned revenue of $4.26 million.
```

In this example, "million" is the main word in the phrase "$4.26 million." The head of "million" is "of," which is a child of "revenue," which, in turn, is a child of "earned," the main verb of the sentence.

Using Context to Improve the Ticket-Booking Chatbot

As you've no doubt realized by now, there's no single solution for all intelligent text-processing tasks. For example, the ticket-booking script shown earlier in this chapter will only find a destination if the submitted sentence contains the word "to."

One way to make these scripts more useful is to take context into account to determine an appropriate response. Let's increase the functionality of the ticket-booking script so it can handle a wider set of user input, including utterances that don't contain a "to + GPE" pair in any combination. For example, look at the following utterance:

```
I am attending the conference in Berlin.
```

Here, the user has expressed an intention to go to Berlin without "to." Only the GPE entity "Berlin" is in the sentence. In such cases, it would be reasonable for a chatbot to ask a confirmatory question, such as the following:

```
You want a ticket to Berlin, right?
```

The improved ticket-booking chatbot should produce different outputs based on three different situations:

- The user expresses a clear intention to book a ticket to a certain destination.
- It's not immediately clear whether the user wants a ticket to the destination mentioned.
- The user doesn't mention any destination.

Depending on which category the user input falls under, the chatbot generates an appropriate response. Figure 6-5 illustrates how to represent this user input handling on a diagram.

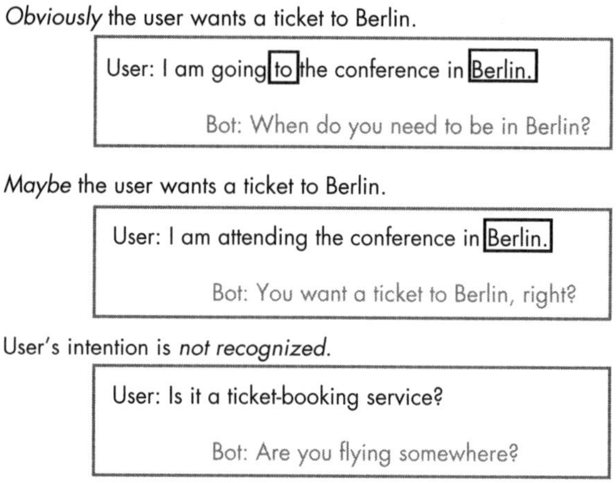

Obviously the user wants a ticket to Berlin.

> User: I am going to the conference in Berlin.
>
> Bot: When do you need to be in Berlin?

Maybe the user wants a ticket to Berlin.

> User: I am attending the conference in Berlin.
>
> Bot: You want a ticket to Berlin, right?

User's intention is *not recognized.*

> User: Is it a ticket-booking service?
>
> Bot: Are you flying somewhere?

Figure 6-5: An example of user input handling in a ticket-booking application

The following script implements this design. For convenience, the code is divided into several parts.

The first snippet contains the guess_destination function, which searches a sentence for a GPE entity. Also, we'll need to insert the dep_destination function defined and discussed in "Iterating Over the Heads of Tokens" on page 87. Recall that this function searches a sentence for the "to + GPE" pattern. We'll need the dep_destination and guess_destination functions to handle the first and second scenarios of user input, respectively.

```
import spacy
nlp = spacy.load('en')
#Insert the dep_destination function from a previous listing here
#...
def guess_destination(doc):
  for token in doc:
 ❶ if token.ent_type != 0 and token.ent_type_ == 'GPE':
    ❷ return token.text
❸ return 'Failed to determine'
```

The code in the guess_destination function iterates over the tokens in a
sentence, looking for a GPE entity ❶. Once it finds one, the function returns
it to the calling code ❷. If it fails to find one, the function returns 'Failed to
determine' ❸, meaning the sentence doesn't contain a GPE entity.

In the gen_function that follows, we generate a response based on what
the functions defined in the preceding snippet return.

```
def gen_response(doc):
❶ dest = det_destination(doc)
  if dest != 'Failed to determine':
  ❷ return 'When do you need to be in ' + dest + '?'
❸ dest = guess_destination(doc)
  if dest != 'Failed to determine':
  ❹ return 'You want a ticket to ' + dest +', right?'
❺ return 'Are you flying somewhere?'
```

The code in the gen_response function starts by invoking the det
_destination function ❶, which determines whether an utterance contains
a "to + GPE" pair. If one is found, we assume that the user wants a ticket to
the destination and they need to clarify their departure time ❷.

If the det_destination function hasn't found a "to + GPE" pair in the utterance, we invoke the guess_destination function ❸. This function tries to find
a GPE entity. If it finds such an entity, it asks the user a confirmatory question
about whether they want to fly to that destination ❹. Otherwise, if it finds
no GPE entity in the utterance, the script asks the user whether they want to
fly somewhere ❺.

To test the code, we apply the pipeline to a sentence and then send the
doc to the gen_response function we used in the previous listing:

```
doc = nlp(u'I am going to the conference in Berlin.')
print(gen_response(doc))
```

For the utterance submitted in this example, you should see the following output:

```
When do you need to be in Berlin?
```

You can experiment with the sample utterance to see different output.

Making a Smarter Chatbot by Finding Proper Modifiers

One way to make your chatbot smarter is to use dependency trees to find modifiers for particular words. For example, you might teach your application to recognize the adjectives that are applicable to a given noun. Then you could tell the bot, "I'd like to read a book," to which the smart bot could respond like this: "Would you like a fiction book?"

A *modifier* is an optional element in a phrase or a clause used to change the meaning of another element. Removing a modifier doesn't typically change the basic meaning of the sentence, but it does make it less specific. As a quick example, consider the following two sentences:

```
I want to read a book.
I want to read a book on Python.
```

The first sentence doesn't use modifiers. The second uses the modifier "on Python," making your request more detailed.

If you want to be specific, you must use modifiers. For example, to generate a proper response to a user, you might need to learn which modifiers you can use in conjunction with a given noun or verb.

Consider the following phrase:

```
That exotic fruit from Africa.
```

In this noun phrase, "fruit" is the head, "that" and "exotic" are *premodifiers*—modifiers located in front of the word being modified—and "from Africa" is a *postmodifier* phrase—a modifier that follows the word it limits or qualifies. Figure 6-6 shows the dependency tree for this phrase.

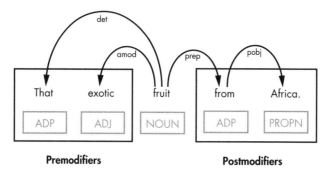

Figure 6-6: An example of premodifiers and postmodifiers

Suppose you want to determine possible adjectival modifiers for the word "fruit." (Adjectival modifiers are always premodifiers.) Also, you want to look at what GPE entities you can find in the postmodifiers of this same word. This information could later help you generate an utterance during a conversation on fruits.

The following script implements this design:

```
import spacy
nlp = spacy.load('en')
❶ doc = nlp(u"Kiwano has jelly-like flesh with a refreshingly fruity taste. This
  is a nice exotic fruit from Africa. It is definitely worth trying.")
❷ fruit_adjectives = []
❸ fruit_origins = []
  for token in doc:
    ❹ if token.text == 'fruit':
       ❺ fruit_adjectives = fruit_adjectives + [modifier.text for modifier in
         token.lefts if modifier.pos_ == 'ADJ']
       ❻ fruit_origins = fruit_origins + [doc[modifier.i + 1].text for modifier
         in token.rights if modifier.text == 'from' and doc[modifier.i + 1].ent
         _type != 0]
  print('The list of adjectival modifiers for word fruit:', fruit_adjectives)
  print('The list of GPE names applicable to word fruit as postmodifiers:',
  fruit_origins)
```

We start by applying the pipeline to a short text that contains the word "fruit" with both premodifiers and postmodifiers ❶. We define two empty lists: fruit_adjectives ❷ and fruit_origins ❸. The first one will hold any adjectival modifiers found for the word "fruit." The second list will hold any GPE entities found among the postmodifiers of "fruit."

Next, in a loop iterating over the tokens of the entire text, we look for the word "fruit" ❹. Once this word is found, we first determine its adjectival premodifiers by picking up its syntactic children to the left and choosing only adjectives (determiners and compounds can also be premodifiers). We append the adjectival modifiers to the fruit_adjectives list ❺.

Then we search for postmodifiers by checking the right-hand syntactic children of the word "fruit." In particular, we look for named entities, and then append them to the fruit_origins list ❻.

The script outputs the following two lists:

```
The list of adjectival modifiers for word fruit: ['nice', 'exotic']
The list of GPE names applicable to word fruit as postmodifiers: ['Africa']
```

Now your bot "knows" that a fruit can be nice, exotic (or both nice and exotic), and might come from Africa.

Summary

When you need to process an utterance, or even just a phrase, it's often important to look at its structure to determine which general patterns it matches. Using spaCy's linguistic features, you can detect these patterns, allowing your script to understand the user's intention and respond properly.

Using patterns based on linguistic features works well when you need to recognize the general structure of a sentence, which involves the subject, modal auxiliary verb, main verb, and direct object. But a real-world application needs to recognize more complicated sentence structures and be prepared for a wider set of user input. This is where the syntactic dependency tree of a sentence becomes very useful. You can walk the dependency tree of a sentence in different ways, extracting necessary pieces of information from it. For example, you can use dependency trees to find modifiers for particular words, and then use this information later to generate intelligent text.

7

VISUALIZATIONS

Perhaps the simplest way to discover insights in data is to represent that data graphically. Visualizations, like the one shown in Figure 7-1, allow you to immediately identify patterns within your data.

In this chapter, you'll learn how to generate visualizations for the syntactic structure of a sentence and the named entities in a document using spaCy's built-in visualizers: the displaCy dependency visualizer and the displaCy named entity visualizer.

We'll start by exploring interactive demos of these visualizers, which are available on the Explosion AI website (Explosion AI is the maker of spaCy), to understand what the spaCy visualizers can accomplish. Next, you'll learn to spin up a displaCy web server on your machine, allowing you to programmatically visualize a Doc object from within spaCy. You'll also learn how to customize your visualizations. Finally, you'll learn how to use displaCy to render manually prepared data without having to pass in a Doc object.

Getting Started with spaCy's Built-In Visualizers

Let's begin by exploring how the displaCy dependency visualizer and the displaCy named entity visualizer work. The quickest way to get started with spaCy's built-in visualizers is to take advantage of their interactive demos available at *https://explosion.ai/demos/*. On this page, you'll find links to the demo pages for the two displaCy visualizers along with some other demo links.

displaCy Dependency Visualizer

The displaCy dependency visualizer generates a syntactic dependency visualization for a submitted text. To use its interactive demo, navigate to *https://explosion.ai/demos/displacy/*. Replace the sample sentence in the "Text to parse" text box with your text, and then click the search icon (magnifying glass) at the right of the box to generate a visualization. The result might look like Figure 7-1.

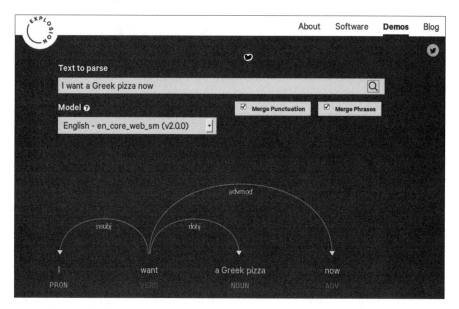

Figure 7-1: The displaCy dependency visualizer on the Explosion AI website

The dependency visualizer shows the part-of-speech tags and syntactic dependencies in a submitted text, displaying its syntactic structure immediately.

The visualizer allows you to customize your graphic with the "Merge Punctuation" and "Merge Phrases" checkboxes. "Merge Punctuation" merges a punctuation mark to the preceding token, making a visualization more compact and therefore more readable. "Merge Phrases" merges each noun phrase into a single token, as shown in the example in Figure 7-1. Both options are set by default.

You can change either or both of these defaults by deselecting the corresponding box or boxes. For example, if you deselect the "Merge Phrases" box for "I want a Greek pizza now," you'll see a more detailed dependency parsing for this sentence that shows you the dependencies within the noun phrase "a Greek pizza."

Keeping the "Merge Phrases" box selected allows you to get a more compact dependency tree, which can be especially useful when dealing with a sentence containing several noun phrases. For example, consider the following sentence: "I see a few young people working in their vegetable field." It contains two noun phrases: "a few young people" and "their vegetable field." The first one is the direct object of the verb "see," and the second is the object of the preposition in the prepositional phrase that modifies the verb "work," showing the dependency labels dobj and pobj, respectively. Strictly speaking, these dependency labels are related to the nouns in the corresponding phrases rather than to an entire sentence.

In addition to the "Merge Punctuation" and "Merge Phrases" options, you can choose a statistical language model to use from the list of available models. This option allows you to try a model for dependency parsing without downloading and installing it in your environment. Currently, you can choose from the following models: en_core_web_sm, en_core_web_md, and en_core_web_lg, as well as small (sm) models for other European languages, such as German, Spanish, Portuguese, French, Italian, and Dutch.

displaCy Named Entity Visualizer

The displaCy named entity visualizer generates a named entity visualization for a submitted text. You'll find its interactive demo at *https://explosion .ai/demos/displacy-ent/*. From a user's standpoint, it works similarly to the displaCy dependency visualizer demo discussed in the previous section. To generate a visualization for a text, enter it into the text box, and then click the search icon. The visualizer will process your query and output an original text at the bottom of the window, highlighting the named entities discovered along with their labels, as shown in Figure 7-2.

You can choose what types of named entities the application should recognize in a submitted text by selecting or deselecting the boxes under "Entity labels". In the example shown in Figure 7-2, you add PERCENT and CARDINAL to the list of entity label types chosen by default. Adding the PERCENT entity type tells the visualizer to recognize phrases expressing a percentage or that include the "%" symbol. Adding the CARDINAL entity type guarantees that the visualizer will recognize phrases related to numerals in the submitted text.

Which boxes you should select depends on your context. When processing a financial report, you might select the MONEY and DATE boxes. But if the report includes records of the financial activities of more than one company, you might also want to select the ORG entity label box to instruct the visualizer to highlight company names in the text.

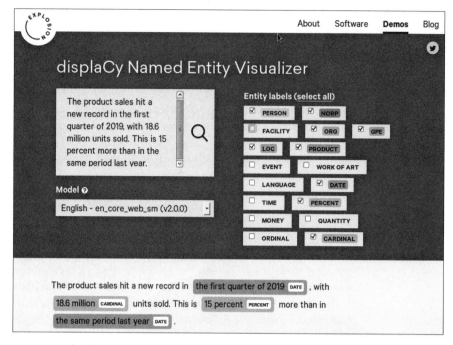

Figure 7-2: The displaCy named entity visualizer on the Explosion AI website

Visualizing from Within spaCy

Starting with spaCy v2.0, the displaCy visualizers are integrated into the core library. This means that you can start using them from within your Python code immediately after installing spaCy.

To do so, you must use the following process: start a built-in web server, and then send a Doc object (or a list of Doc objects) to it for rendering. The server will generate a visualization for the submitted Doc, which you can then view in your browser. We'll walk through several examples in this section.

Visualizing Dependency Parsing

The following script shows the simplest way to generate a dependency tree visualization for a sentence:

```
  import spacy
  nlp = spacy.load('en')
❶ doc = nlp(u"I want a Greek pizza.")
❷ from spacy import displacy
❸ displacy.serve(doc, ❹style='dep')
```

We create a Doc object to submit to displaCy ❶. Then we import the displaCy library from the core library ❷, after which we can start a displaCy web server, passing the Doc object to it. Both operations are done by calling the display.serve() method ❸. By setting parameter style to 'dep', we instruct displaCy to use the dependency visualizer ❹, generating a dependency tree visualization for the text in the Doc object. If you're interested in implementing the checkbox options explored earlier in this chapter, reference "Try This" on page 104.

Whether you run this code in a Python session or as a separate script, the execution enters an infinite loop and shows messages from the displaCy web server. The initial messages you should see are the following:

```
Serving on port 5000...
Using the 'dep' visualizer
```

This means that the server has generated a dependency tree visualization for the submitted text and serves HTTP requests on port 5000 (the default port) on your host. In practical terms, this means you can point your browser to *http://localhost:5000* to view the visualization. In this example, it should look like Figure 7-3.

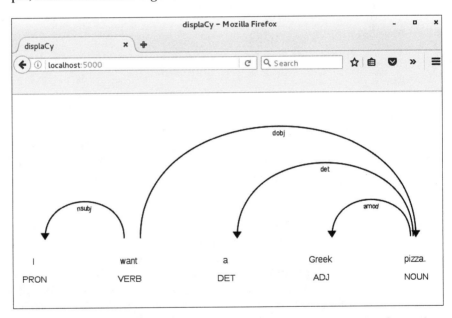

Figure 7-3: An example of a dependency tree visualization you can generate from within your Python code and then view in your browser

To shut down the displaCy server, enter CTRL-C in the terminal in which you executed the script that started the server. As a result, you should see the following final message from the server:

```
Shutting down server on port 5000.
```

After shutting down the server, you won't be able to generate a new copy of the visualization in your browser, but you'll be able to view the copies you've already generated.

Try This

Try using the named entity visualizer by altering the script for the dependency visualizer in the previous section. To instruct displaCy to apply the named entity visualizer, set the `display.serve()` method's style parameter to `'ent'`.

To produce a more interesting visualization, you might use longer text containing, perhaps, more than one sentence. For example, try using the following text:

```
Microsoft Windows is a family of proprietary operating systems developed and
sold by Microsoft. Bill Gates announced Microsoft Windows on November 10,
1983. Microsoft first released Windows for sale on November 20, 1985. Windows
1.0 was initially sold for $100.00, and its sales surpassed 500,000 copies in
April 1987. For comparison, more than a million copies of Windows 95 were sold
in just the first 4 days.
```

After calling the `display.serve()` method on the Doc object, point your browser to *http://localhost:5000* to view the visualization. Pay attention to the named entities and their types recognized by the entity recognizer in this sample text. In particular, you should see that the entity recognizer finds the names of persons, products, and companies, as well as phrases related to dates, numbers, and money.

Sentence-by-Sentence Visualizations

Visualizing dependency trees works fine when you're working with a single sentence. But the graphics can get long and space consuming when you're visualizing a long text, making them difficult to read when displayed in one row. Although displaCy generates separate visualizations for each sentence, when you pass in a Doc containing more than one sentence, it lays them out in a single row.

Instead of passing in a Doc object, you might want to visualize sentence-by-sentence. For example, this might be useful when you need to extract the meaning from an entire discourse and want to explore a sequence of sentences. Starting with version 2.0.12, displaCy allows you to pass in Span objects and then lays out the visualizations in rows. You can pass in a list of `doc.sents` if you want to create one visualization for each sentence found in `doc.sents`, as shown in the following code:

```
import spacy
nlp = spacy.load('en')
doc = nlp(u"I have a relaxed pair of jeans. Now I want a skinny pair.")
❶ spans = list(doc.sents)
from spacy import display
display.serve(❷spans, style='dep')
```

As discussed in Chapter 3, the Doc object's `doc.sents` property is an iterator over the sentences in a Doc object. For this reason, you can't use this property to refer to sentences by index, but you can iterate over them in a loop or create a list of Span objects where each span represents a sentence. In this code, we convert the sentences in the Doc into a list of Span objects ❶. Then we pass in that spans list to `display.serve()` to visualize ❷.

This should generate one visualization for each sentence, laid out in rows, allowing you to view them by scrolling vertically.

Customizing Your Visualizations with the Options Argument

In addition to the docs and style arguments that you saw in the examples so far, the `display.serve()` method can take several other arguments. The `options` argument is perhaps one of the most interesting because it allows you to define a dictionary of settings to customize the layout of the visualization. We'll cover some of the most useful `options` settings in this section.

Using Dependency Visualizer Options

Long sentences can be difficult to view when they're displayed in one row. In such cases, you can create visualizations in *compact mode*, which takes less space. For that you need to set the `'compact'` option to `True` in the `options` argument, as illustrated in this script. The script also changes the font that the visualizer uses. (The entire list of available options in the displaCy API documentation is at *https://spacy.io/api/top-level/#options-dep/*.)

```
import spacy
nlp = spacy.load('en')
doc = nlp(u"I want a Greek pizza.")
from spacy import display
options = {❶'compact': True, ❷'font': 'Tahoma'}
display.serve(doc, style='dep', ❸options=options)
```

The `display.serve()` method expects the `options` argument to be a dictionary. In this example, we set only two options: the `'compact'` option to `True` ❶ and the `'font'` option to `'Tahoma'` ❷, changing their defaults in both cases. (The visualizer lets you use most standard web fonts, such as Arial, Courier, and so on.) We then pass the dictionary of options in as the `options` argument ❸.

Figure 7-4 shows what your browser should display when you point it to *http://localhost:5000* after running the script.

The square arcs you see in the figure might look unusual, but they make the overall visualization more compact, which often can spare you from having to scroll to see the entire diagram.

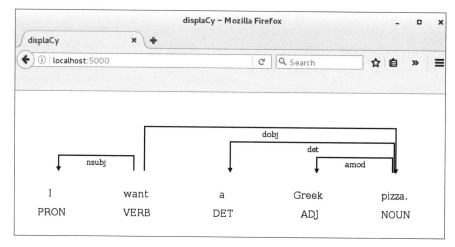

Figure 7-4: An example of a customized dependency visualization

Try This

In the dependency visualizer's interactive demo discussed in "displaCy Dependency Visualizer" on page 98, you used the "Merge Phrases" and "Merge Punctuation" options. In spaCy, you can merge noun phrases into one token with the collapse_phrases option (Figure 7-1 shows the equivalent option on the displaCy visualizer website.), which is set to False by default. The collapse_punct option, which is responsible for attaching punctuation to tokens, is set to True by default.

Change the code in the previous script so it sets the collapse_phrases option to True in the set of passed-in options. Run the script, and then view the generated visualization in your browser to make sure the noun phrases are displayed as a single token.

Using Named Entity Visualizer Options

The list of named entity visualizer options (available at *https://spacy.io/api/ top-level/#displacy_options-ent/*) is much shorter than the list of dependency visualizer options. When using the entity visualizer, you can choose which entity types to highlight with the 'ents' option and override default colors with the 'colors' option.

The first option is the more important of the two, because it allows you to instruct the visualizer to highlight entities of selected types only. The following example illustrates a case when you might want to limit the entity types that the visualizer displays.

In this script, we don't provide any options for the entity visualizer, which means it will highlight entities of all types in the submitted Doc.

```
import spacy
nlp = spacy.load('en')
doc = nlp(u"In 2011, Google launched Google +, its fourth foray into social
networking.")
```

```
❶ doc.user_data['title'] = "An example of an entity visualization"
from spacy import displacy
displacy.serve(doc, style=❷'ent')
```

We use the Doc's user_data attribute to set a title for the Doc ❶. The displaCy visualizer automatically puts the text in this attribute as a headline for the visualization. Adding a title to a visualization is optional but can be useful when you need to annotate your visualizations.

We set the style parameter of displacy.serve() to 'ent' ❷, instructing displaCy to use the named entity visualizer. The resulting visualization should look like the one in Figure 7-5 (although these images are in grayscale, the website uses color).

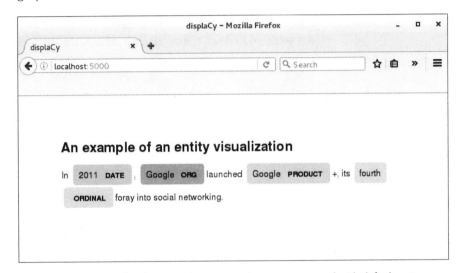

Figure 7-5: An example of a named entity visualization generated with default options

The visualization looks fine in general. But in this context, highlighting the ordinal number "fourth" is probably unnecessary. It's hard to figure out why we might need to extract that information in this context. With the 'ents' option, we select the entity types that we want the visualizer to highlight. The following code illustrates how to implement this. To see how it works, we replace the last line of code in the previous script with the following two lines of code, and then run the updated script:

```
options = {❶'ents': ["ORG", "PRODUCT", "DATE"], ❷'colors': {"ORG": "aqua",
"PRODUCT": "aqua"}}
displacy.serve(doc, style='ent', options=options)
```

This time, the visualizer shouldn't recognize any entities except for those that are of the ORG, PRODUCT, or DATE type ❶. This example also illustrates the use of the 'colors' option that allows us to change the default colors assigned to entity types. In this example, we map the ORG and PRODUCT types to the color "aqua" ❷.

Using the `colors` option, you can map entity types to web color names or hex color codes. In the example on page 105, using the hex code "#00FFFF" would be equal to using the color name "aqua".

Figure 7-6 illustrates what the resulting visualization should look like.

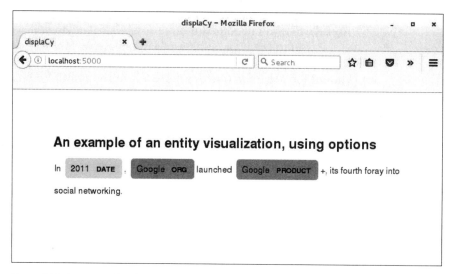

Figure 7-6: An example of an entity visualization generated with the `ents` and `colors` options specified

As you can see, this visualization is almost identical to the one shown in Figure 7-5. But this time the visualizer doesn't highlight the entity of type ORDINAL, because the `ents` option list we've passed in doesn't include this type.

Exporting a Visualization to a File

In the examples so far, we've used the displaCy web server to view the visualizations being generated. As you learned in these examples, you can open the visualization generated with the display.serve() method in your browser as long as the server started with this same invocation of display .serve() is running.

Using the display.render() method, you can avoid this limitation and create a visualization for later use. The display.render() method allows you to render the markup wrapped as an HTML page and then save it in a separate file. Later, you can open this file in any browser without having to invoke a web browser.

The following script shows how to use the display.render() method for the named entity visualization shown in Figure 7-5:

```
import spacy
nlp = spacy.load('en')
```

```
doc = nlp(u"In 2011, Google launched Google +, its fourth foray into social
networking.")
❶ doc.user_data["title"] = "An example of an entity visualization"
#In the next block, you instruct displaCy to render the markup wrapped as a
full HTML page.
from spacy import displacy
❷ html = displacy.render(doc, style='ent', ❸page=True)
#In the next block, you save the html file generated by displacy.render() to
disk on your machine.
❹ from pathlib import Path
❺ output_path = Path("/visualizations/ent_visual.html")
❻ output_path.open("w", encoding="utf-8").write(html)
```

We can divide the code in this script into three parts, each of which
begins with a comment line. The first block should be familiar. Here, we
create a text processing pipeline and then apply it to a text. Then we use
the Doc's user_data attribute to set a headline for the Doc ❶.

In the second block, we render a named entity visualization for the Doc
created in the previous step, using the displacy.render() method ❷. Unlike
displacy.serve(), displacy.render() doesn't run a web server but generates the
HTML markup for a visualization. By setting the page argument to True, we
instruct displacy.render() to generate the markup wrapped as a full HTML
page ❸.

In the final block, we import the Path class from the pathlib module
introduced in Python 3.4 ❹. We can use Path to perform system calls on path
objects. In this example, we instantiate this class on the following path:
/visualizations/ent_visual.html ❺, assuming we already have the */visualizations*
folder available in our local filesystem (otherwise, an exception is thrown).
Then we open the *ent_visual.html* file (it will be created if it doesn't already
exist) in the */visualizations* folder and write the HTML page generated in
the previous step to it ❻.

To sum up, this script generates an HTML file containing a named
entity visualization for the submitted text and saves that file in your filesystem. If you move to the folder where the file has been saved and double-
click the file, it opens in your browser.

Using displaCy to Manually Render Data

The displaCy visualizers allow you to manually create a dataset that you can
then render rather than passing in data as either a doc or span. This can
be useful when you need, for example, to visualize output from other NLP
libraries or when you need to create a visualization using a set of custom tags
or custom dependency labels. (I'll discuss how to make these custom tags
and labels in Chapter 10.)

As an example, let's manually render the sentence "I want a Greek pizza."

Formatting the Data

To begin with, you need to put your data in displaCy's format: a dictionary containing two lists: "words" and "arcs", as illustrated in the following code:

```
sent = {
    "words": [
 ❶  {"text": "I", "tag": "PRON"},
        {"text": "want", "tag": "VERB"},
        {"text": "a", "tag": "DET"},
        {"text": "Greek", "tag": "ADJ"},
        {"text": "pizza", "tag": "NOUN"}
    ],
    "arcs": [
 ❷  {"start": 0, "end": 1, "label": "nsubj", "dir": "left"},
        {"start": 2, "end": 4, "label": "det", "dir": "left"},
        {"start": 3, "end": 4, "label": "amod", "dir": "left"},
        {"start": 1, "end": 4, "label": "dobj", "dir": "right"}
    ]
}
```

The sent dictionary contains two lists: "words" and "arcs", each of which, in turn, includes a set of dictionaries. A dictionary in the "words" list assigns a tag to a certain token in the sentence ❶, and a dictionary in the "arcs" list defines an arc in the dependency tree, connecting two syntactically related words in the sentence ❷. In this example, five words are in the sentence and four syntactic relations are defined on them. That's why the dictionary contains five items in the "words" list and four items in the "arcs" list.

Now that we have a dictionary with the data, we need to generate a dependency parsing visualization for the sample sentence; we can use the following code to render it:

```
❶ from spacy import displacy
displacy.serve(❷sent, style="dep", ❸manual=True)
```

Note that we don't have to import the entire spaCy library. All we need to do is import the display module from it ❶. Then we invoke the displacy .serve() method, passing in the sent dictionary as the first parameter in place of a Doc object ❷. The third parameter, manual, tells displaCy that we created the dataset for rendering manually ❸, so displaCy doesn't need to extract the data from a Doc object.

Try This

When you choose to manually create a dictionary with data to render into a visualization, you can use custom tags, specifying, for example, that the visualizer should use fine-grained part-of-speech tags instead of the coarse-grained tags used by default.

You could accomplish this task by simply setting the fine_grained option to True when passing in a Doc object for rendering, but for practice, try to implement this manually.

In the example from "Formatting the Data" on page 108, change the tags in the "words" list of the "sent" dictionary so their values are fine-grained tags. Next, start the displaCy server and instruct it to generate a visualization based on the data specified in the "sent" dictionary. Then point your browser to *http://localhost:5000* to view the visualization.

Summary

You've seen syntactic structure visualizations in previous chapters, but in this chapter, you learned how to generate those visualizations using the displaCy dependency visualizer. You also learned to generate graphics of named entity information with the displaCy named entity visualizer.

8

INTENT RECOGNITION

A chatbot should be smart enough to understand a user's needs. For example, a conversational chatbot must recognize a user's intent to properly sustain a conversation with the user, and a food-ordering chatbot needs to understand a customer's intent to take an order. Although the task of intent recognition was touched on in previous chapters, this chapter discusses it in more depth.

You'll start by recognizing a user's intent by extracting the transitive verb and direct object of an utterance. Then you'll explore how to derive a user's intent from a sequence of sentences, recognize synonyms for different possible intents, and determine a user's intent using semantic similarity.

Extracting the Transitive Verb and Direct Object for Intent Recognition

You can typically recognize a user's intent in three steps: parsing the sentence into tokens, connecting the tokens with labeled arcs representing syntactic relations, and navigating the arcs to extract the relevant tokens. In many cases, extracting the sentence's transitive verb and direct object can identify the user's intent, as shown by the syntactic dependency parsing in Figure 8-1.

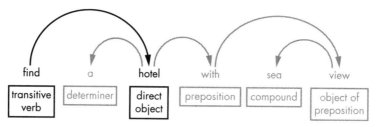

Figure 8-1: An example of a graphical representation of a sentence's syntactic structure

The arc connecting the transitive verb with the direct object indicates that the user's intent is finding a hotel, or just findHotel, if you merged the transitive verb and the direct object into a single word. You could use this structure as an *intent identifier* in a later part of a program, as in the following code fragment:

```
intent = extract_intent(doc)
if intent == 'orderPizza':
  print('We need you to answer some questions to place your order.')
  ...
elif intent == 'showPizza':
  print('Would you like to look at our menu?')
  ...
```

NOTE   *In Chapter 11, you'll see more detailed examples of how to use intent identifiers in a chatbot app's code.*

But sometimes finding the meaning from the transitive verb/direct object pair isn't so easy. You might need to explore the transitive verb and direct object's syntactic relations to find the verb and noun that best describe the intent.

In other situations, a user's intent isn't expressed explicitly, so you must figure out an implied intent. In this section, you'll learn strategies for extracting intent using the syntactic dependency structure.

Obtaining the Transitive Verb/Direct Object Pair

Let's start by extracting the transitive verb/direct object pair from a sentence by checking the dependency label of each token, looking for dobj. Once we find the direct object, we can easily get the corresponding transitive verb by obtaining the syntactic head of the direct object, as illustrated in the following script:

```
import spacy
nlp = spacy.load('en')
❶ doc = nlp(u'show me the best hotel in berlin')
❷ for token in doc:
    if token.dep_ == 'dobj':
        print(❸token.head.text + token.text.capitalize())
```

In this script, we apply the pipeline to a sample sentence ❶ and then iterate over the tokens, searching for the one whose dependency label is dobj ❷. When it's found, we determine the corresponding transitive verb by obtaining the direct object's head ❸. In this example, we also concatenate the transitive verb and its direct object to express the intent in the form of a single word.

The script generates the following string:

```
showHotel
```

Keep in mind that not all sentences containing a transitive verb/direct object pair express intent. For example, "He gave me a book" is just a statement of fact. We could filter out such sentences by checking the verb's characteristics, picking up only those sentences whose verbs are in the present tense and not third person. Still, it would be uncommon to hear a sentence like that from a customer talking to a chatbot that takes orders for a business.

Extracting Multiple Intents with token.conjuncts

Sometimes, you might find a sentence that seems to express more than one intent. For example, consider the following sentence:

```
I want a pizza and cola.
```

In this scenario, a user wants to order a pizza and a cola. But in most cases, you can consider these intents part of a single complex intent. Although a user requests items of different types, you'd typically treat this sentence as a single order consisting of several items. In this example, you might recognize the intent as orderPizza, formed by combining the transitive verb and direct object pair, but extract pizza and cola as items for the order being placed.

Figure 8-2 shows the dependency tree for the sample sentence.

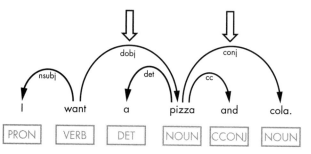

Figure 8-2: The dependency tree of a sentence containing a direct object and its conjunct

In the diagram, you can see two arrows pointing to the arcs for the direct object "pizza" and the conjunct "cola" associated with it. The *conjunct* of a noun is another noun that is joined to it by a conjunction, such as "and," "or," and so on. To extract the direct object and the conjunct associated with it, we can use the following code:

```
doc = nlp(u'I want a pizza and cola.')
#extract the direct object and the conjunct associated with it
for token in doc:
  if token.dep_ == 'dobj':
    dobj = [token.text]
    conj = [t.text for t in ❶token.conjuncts]
#compose the list of the extracted elements
❷ dobj_conj = dobj + conj
print(dobj_conj)
```

We extract the conjunct associated with the direct object using the conjuncts property of the Token object used for the direct object ❶. Once we've obtained the direct object and its conjuncts, we combine them into a single list ❷.

The script output should be as follows:

```
['pizza', 'cola']
```

To compose the intent, we should extract the verb, too. The simplest way to obtain it when we already have the direct object is to obtain the direct object's syntactic head (you saw an example of this in "Obtaining the Transitive Verb/Direct Object Pair" on page 113):

```
verb = dobj.head
```

Then, using the text property of the verb and the direct object, we can compose the intent.

Try This

In the script provided in on page 114, you accessed the conjunct linked to the direct object through the Token object's conjuncts property. In a new script, replace that line with code that extracts the conjunct by finding the arc labeled conj moving outward from the direct object. You can do this within the same loop in which you obtain the direct object by finding the arc labeled dobj. Be sure to check that the head of the conj arc matches the direct object.

Using Word Lists to Extract the Intent

In some cases, tokens other than the transitive verb and direct object best describe the user's intent. These tokens are typically related to the transitive verb or direct object. So you'll need to go a step further and explore the transitive verb and direct object's syntactic relations to discover the words that best formulate the intent.

As an example, consider the following utterance:

```
I want to place an order for a pizza.
```

In this sentence, the words "want" and "pizza" best describe the intent, but neither word is a direct object or transitive verb. However, looking at the utterance's dependency tree, you'll see that "want" and "pizza" are related to the transitive verb "place" and the direct object "order," respectively. Figure 8-3 shows the dependency tree discussed here.

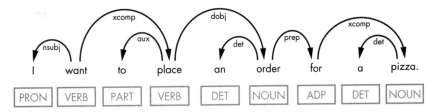

Figure 8-3: The dependency tree of an utterance whose transitive verb and direct object don't convey the user's intent

To extract these words from the utterance, we'll use a list of predefined words, and then search the user's utterance for those words.

An experienced programmer might call into question the effectiveness of hardcoding such a list, because it can be quite long, especially if used in many different contexts. But if the list is intended for a specific context, say, ordering pizza, it can be surprisingly short, which makes this approach very efficient. The following code implements this approach:

```
#apply the pipeline to the sample sentence
doc = nlp(u'I want to place an order for a pizza.')
# extract the direct object and its transitive verb
dobj = ''
```

```
    tverb = ''
    for token in doc:
❶   if token.dep_ == 'dobj':
        dobj = token
        tverb = token.head
    # extract the verb for the intent's definition
    intentVerb = ''
    verbList = ['want', 'like', 'need', 'order']
❷   if tverb.text in verbList:
        intentVerb = tverb
❸   else:
        if tverb.head.dep_ == 'ROOT':
            intentVerb = tverb.head
    # extract the object for the intent's definition
    intentObj = ''
    objList = ['pizza', 'cola']
❹   if dobj.text in objList:
        intentObj = dobj
    else:
        for child in dobj.children:
            if child.dep_ == 'prep':
❺             intentObj = list(child.children)[0]
                break
❻           elif child.dep_ == 'compound':
                intentObj = child
                break
    # print the intent expressed in the sample sentence
    print(intentVerb.text + intentObj.text.capitalize())
```

As always, we start by finding and extracting the direct object and its transitive verb ❶. Once we've obtained them, we check whether they can be found in the corresponding lists of predefined words. Here, we use simplified lists, of course: the verbList list contains the verbs a customer might use to place an order, and the objList contains direct objects that are possible menu items. We start by checking the transitive verb ❷. If it's not in the list of allowed verbs ❸, we check the main verb (ROOT) of the sentence, which is the head of the transitive verb. If the transitive verb is the main verb of the sentence, this implementation will work anyway, because the head of the main verb (ROOT) refers to itself.

Next, we move on to checking the direct object ❹. If it's not in the list of allowed words, we check its syntactic children. We start by checking the preposition of the direct object. If it exists, we pick up the preposition's child (it can have only one child) ❺, which is always the object of the preposition.

To make this approach applicable to a wider variety of cases, it's not enough to just check for prepositions in the direct object's children. For example, this logic wouldn't work for the following utterance: "I want to place a pizza order," where there is no preposition child branch. Instead, the direct object has a left child, "pizza," which spaCy tags as a compound. Therefore, we check for compounds in the direct object's children ❻.

Finally, we print the string representing the intent identifier. We should get the following string:

```
wantPizza
```

Notice that we use `wantPizza` as the intent identifier instead of `placeOrder` (which we would have gotten if we'd simply used the transitive verb/direct object pair). This approach allows us to reduce the number of intent identifiers used in the application.

Finding the Meanings of Words Using Synonyms and Semantic Similarity

English, like many other natural languages, lets you express the same thoughts and intents in different ways, because it contains *synonyms*—words or phrases that mean nearly the same thing.

As a developer of a chatbot application, you need to account for the fact that your users might use a fairly wide set of phrases for each intent the application is supposed to support. This means that your application must recognize synonymous phrases in user input. In fact, if you're building your chatbot on a popular bot platform, such as Google's Dialogflow, you're required to submit a set of phrases for each possible intent. You then use these utterances behind the scenes to train the bot's model.

There's more than one approach to recognizing synonyms. One option is to use a set of predefined lists of synonyms. You check a word of interest against those lists, recognizing the word's meaning based on the list in which it was found. Another option is to recognize synonyms based on semantic similarity, a task described in Chapter 5 in detail. I discuss both approaches in the following sections.

Recognizing Synonyms Using Predefined Lists

You already know that, in most cases, the transitive verb and its direct object best describe the intent of a phrase. A simple way to recognize whether two phrases express the same intent is to make sure the transitive verbs in both phrases are synonymous and their direct objects are synonyms as well.

For example, the following three sentences express the same intent, which you might define as `orderPizza`:

```
I want a dish. I'd like to order a pizza. Give me a pie.
```

To process these utterances, you use the following steps:

1. Perform dependency parsing to extract a transitive verb and its direct object from a sentence.
2. Check with the predefined lists of synonyms to replace the transitive verb and the direct object with words that the application recognizes.
3. Compose the string that represents the intent.

The diagram in Figure 8-4 summarizes these steps, illustrating how this might work for, say, "I want a dish."

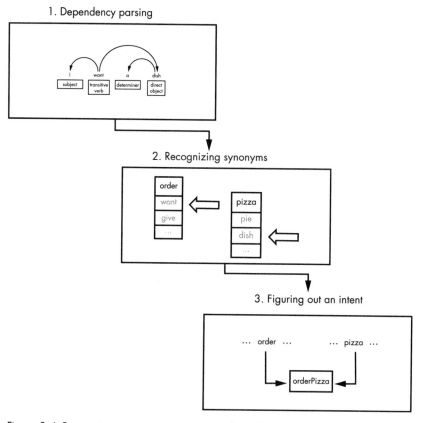

Figure 8-4: Processing intent recognition using lists of synonyms

After dependency parsing (done implicitly when you apply the pipeline to an utterance), you extract the direct object and the transitive verb, and then check them against the corresponding list of synonyms. If you find a match, you replace the word with the one that tops the list, which the application should recognize.

Let's examine what a Python implementation of this scenario might look like:

```
#apply the pipeline to the sample sentence
doc = nlp(u'I want a dish.')
#extract the transitive verb and its direct object from the dependency tree
❶ for token in doc:
    if token.dep_ == 'dobj':
      verb = token.head.text
      dobj = token.text
#create a list of tuples for possible verb synonyms
❷ verbList = [('order','want','give','make'),('show','find')]
    #find the tuple containing the transitive verb extracted from the sample
❸ verbSyns = [item for item in verbList if verb in item]
```

```
#create a list of tuples for possible direct object synonyms
❹ dobjList = [('pizza','pie','dish'),('cola','soda')]
#find the tuple containing the direct object extracted from the sample
dobjSyns = [item for item in dobjList if dobj in item]
#replace the transitive verb and the direct object with synonyms supported by
the application
#and compose the string that represents the intent
❺ intent = verbSyns[0][0] + dobjSyns[0][0].capitalize()
print(intent)
```

We start by creating a Doc object instance for the sample sentence. Then we iterate over the dependency tree available through the Doc object, extracting the transitive verb and its direct object ❶. Next, we create a list of tuples containing all allowable transitive verbs along with their synonyms ❷. The first element in each tuple contains a transitive verb that the application can recognize, and the other elements in the tuple are its synonyms.

Now that we've defined the allowable transitive verbs and their synonyms and put them all in a list of tuples, we can loop over the entire list to find a tuple that contains the transitive verb extracted from the sample sentence ❸.

Similarly, we create a list of tuples for the recognized direct objects and their synonyms, and then find the tuple containing the direct object extracted from the sample ❹.

Finally, we concatenate the first elements of the chosen tuples to compose the intent name ❺. As a result, the print command should output the following string:

```
orderPizza
```

Keep in mind that the set of synonyms to choose for a given verb depends largely on the type of application we're creating. For example, in the context of a bot application that takes pizza orders, the verbs "make" and "give" can be considered synonymous. The reason is that users might interchangeably use the phrases "Make me a pizza" and "Give me a pizza" when ordering a pizza.

Try This

Use the sample code provided on page 118 as the basis for creating a new script. Make the script retain the original functionality but generate "unrecognized" as the intent name when the transitive verb, its direct object, or both can't be found in the respective lists. To test your code, experiment with the sample sentence, changing it so the new functionality can be seen in action. For example, you might use the following sentence:

```
I want an apple.
```

Test it with a sentence containing a verb that isn't included in the list.

Also, you might try to handle the conjunction problem discussed in the previous sections using synonym lists.

Recognizing Implied Intents Using Semantic Similarity

Real-world implementations will likely include more complex logic than you've seen in the examples provided in this chapter so far. Even using a large set of predefined lists of synonyms won't always work. The reason is that users express their intentions in many different ways, and they don't always do so explicitly.

Recognizing an implied intent depends heavily on the context. For example, if your bot is designed for a specific type of task, say, ordering food, it should recognize phrases that imply a request, such as "I feel like eating a pie.", as the intention to place a pizza order.

One widely known technique to make the user express their intent more clearly is asking clarifying questions. To determine what question to ask, you can calculate the semantic similarity of the previous user utterance.

Figure 8-5 illustrates how to implement this task.

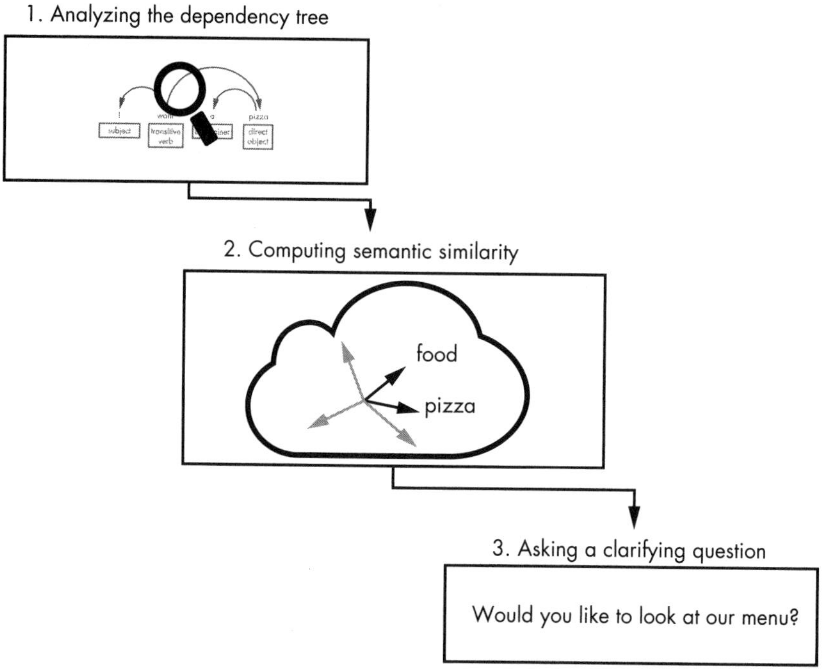

Figure 8-5: Recognizing an implied intent by calculating semantic similarity and asking clarifying questions

You start by analyzing the dependency tree of the input utterance to extract the direct object and its transitive verb. If, for example, the direct object can't be found in the predefined list of synonyms, as discussed in

"Recognizing Synonyms Using Predefined Lists" on page 117, you might try to determine how similar the direct object is to the words included in the list. Based on the results of calculating semantic similarity, you can then generate a clarifying user question.

Let's implement this technique in code, which I'll break up into sections. As usual, we start with applying the text-processing pipeline to the sample sentence:

```
doc = nlp(u'I feel like eating a pie.')
```

Then we extract the direct object token:

```
for token in doc:
  if token.dep_ == 'dobj':
    dobj = token
```

We create a token for the word "food." We'll calculate the semantic similarity between this token and the direct object token:

```
tokens = nlp(u'food')
```

If the level of similarity is greater than a predefined threshold, the application guesses that the user is most likely interested in placing an order. Then it asks a clarifying question to confirm this:

```
if dobj.similarity(tokens[0]) > 0.6:
  question = 'Would you like to look at our menu?'
```

Recall from Chapter 5 that spaCy uses word vectors to calculate the semantic similarity of tokens. The closer two vectors are in the vector space, the higher the level of similarity is between them. In this example, we use 0.6 as the minimum degree of similarity required to assume the direct object resembles a food product.

Try This

Of course, you won't know in advance which phrases the user will use and how easy it will be to recognize the user's intent. Neither will your application. That's why real-world applications typically combine several approaches to recognize intent. Combine the approach based on recognizing synonyms with the approach based on handling implied intents, discussed in the previous sections, so you can handle more possible situations. Start by trying to extract the intent from an utterance using the synonyms-based approach. Then, if that fails, try the approach based on using semantic similarity. If both approaches fail, you might label the utterance as expressing an unrecognized intent.

Extracting Intent from a Sequence of Sentences

In a discourse, the words reflecting a user's intent might appear across different sentences, as in the following example:

```
I have finished my pizza. I want another one.
```

Your bot should be ready to handle this scenario by extracting a user's intent from an entire discourse. In this section, I'll walk you through a technique for doing this.

Walking the Dependency Structures of a Discourse

Let's start by looking at the dependency parsing for the discourse, which will disclose the transitive verb/direct object pairs in each sentence, as shown in Figure 8-6.

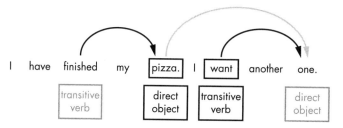

Figure 8-6: A visual representation of the dependency parsing of the entire discourse

The pale arrow in the diagram represents the dependency of interest. In other words, you want to replace the substitute "one" with the noun "pizza" it stands for. But the dependency parser in spaCy doesn't show this link because it can't connect tokens from different sentences. So the task of determining these dependencies is left to you.

Replacing Proforms with Their Antecedents

An *antecedent* is an expression (such as a word or clause) that gives its meaning to a *proform* (such as a pronoun or pro-verb). In this kind of intent extraction, you'll have to determine the antecedents and replace the corresponding proforms with them. You can do so using the following steps:

1. Parse the dependencies of the entire discourse.
2. Dissect the discourse into sentences.
3. Find the antecedent for the pronoun that is the direct object of the transitive verb to be used in the intent definition.

Figure 8-7 shows these steps diagrammatically.

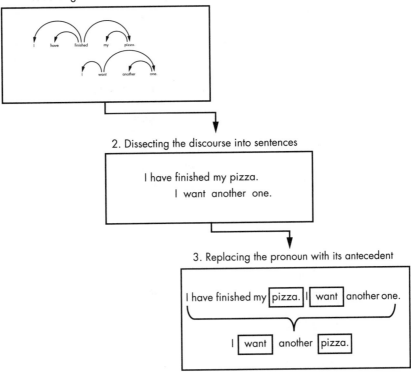

1. Parsing of the entire discourse

I have finished my pizza.

I want another one.

2. Dissecting the discourse into sentences

I have finished my pizza.
I want another one.

3. Replacing the pronoun with its antecedent

I have finished my pizza. I want another one.

I want another pizza.

Figure 8-7: A graphical depiction of extracting intent from a sequence of sentences

In spaCy, we can implement the first two steps with a couple lines of code:

```
doc = nlp(u'I have finished my pizza. I want another one.')
```

We convert the object that the `doc.sents` property returns into a list so we can refer to each sentence in the text by its index. (We could also directly iterate over a sequence of sentences contained in `doc.sents` using a for loop.)

Next, we define two lists containing the allowable transitive verbs and allowable direct objects, respectively:

```
verbList = [('order','want','give','make'),('show','find')]
dobjList = [('pizza','pie','pizzaz'),('cola','soda')]
```

These lists contain tuples of synonyms (refer to "Recognizing Synonyms Using Predefined Lists" on page 117 for details).

We also need to define a list for allowable substitutes. To do so, we must determine what proforms the direct object could be. Let's first figure out what other phrases we could use in place of the last sentence, and then highlight the direct object in each phrase. Possible alternatives include the following:

I want another **one**. I want **it** again. I want the **same**. I want **more**.

So, we can define the substitute list as follows:

```
substitutes = ('one','it','same','more')
```

Unlike the transitive verb and direct object lists, the substitute list has a simple structure, because we don't need to group substitutes. The same substitute could refer to any of the direct objects.

In addition to the lists, we might want to define a dictionary to hold the intent definition parts as they're being extracted:

```
intent = {'verb': '', 'dobj': ''}
```

Now we're ready to start the intent recognition process:

```
for sent in doc.sents:
  for token in sent:
    if token.dep_ == 'dobj':
      verbSyns = [item for item in verbList if token.head.text in item]
❶    dobjSyns = [item for item in dobjList if token.text in item]
      substitute =  [item for item in substitutes if token.text in item]
      if ❷(dobjSyns != [] or substitute != []) and ❸verbSyns != []:
          intent['verb'] = verbSyns[0][0]
❹    if dobjSyns != []:
          intent['dobj'] = dobjSyns[0][0]
```

The outer loop iterates over the sequence of sentences held in the Doc object. The inner loop, in turn, iterates over the tokens found in a sentence. We check each token to see whether it's a direct object. If it is, we determine whether the direct object is part of either the direct object synonyms list or the substitutes list ❶. We also check whether the corresponding transitive verb is in the transitive verb synonyms list.

We extract the direct object only if it's in either the direct object synonyms list or the substitutes list ❷. For example, we wouldn't be interested in extracting the transitive verb from the following phrase (unless we sell apples, of course):

I want an apple.

Nor are we interested in a transitive verb if it's not in the allowable list ❸, even if its direct object satisfies this condition, as in the following phrase:

I like it.

That's why, before picking up the transitive verb, we check not only whether the direct object is in either the direct object synonyms list or the substitutes list, but also whether the transitive verb is in the transitive verb synonyms list.

Finally, to pick up the direct object that defines the intent, we make sure we can find it in the direct object synonyms list ❹. Now we can compose the intent definition:

```
intentStr = intent['verb'] + intent['dobj'].capitalize()
```

Optionally, we might want to print it to make sure everything works as expected:

```
print(intentStr)
```

We should get the following output:

```
orderPizza
```

This result indicates that the user intends to order a pizza.

Try This

In some discourses, several sentences might separate an antecedent from its proform. For example, consider the following sequence of sentences:

```
I have finished my pizza. It was delicious. I want another one.
```

Edit the script provided on page 124 so it can handle this or a similar sequence of sentences.

Summary

Intent recognition is a complex task that might require you to combine several approaches. In this chapter, you learned how to extract the most important parts of an utterance's dependency tree for intent recognition. Then you analyzed them using predefined lists, semantic similarity, or both approaches. You also extracted the intent from a sequence of sentences by replacing proforms with their antecedents.

9

STORING USER INPUT IN A DATABASE

Many applications designed for business need to transfer the data they work with to a database at some point. For example, a food-ordering chatbot might save an order form after filling it out using the information extracted from dialogue with a customer. Once the order appears in the database, it becomes available for further processing, and the product is eventually shipped to the customer.

This chapter discusses how you can turn information extracted from submitted text into a structured format so you can store and manipulate it within a *relational* (row-and-column) database. Through examples, you'll learn how a chatbot can shred input text into pieces and compose a ready-for-database structure from it.

Converting Unstructured Data into Structured Data

Structured data is organized using a predefined data schema in a formatted repository. If you've worked with relational databases before, you know you must first convert any data you'll enter in the database into a structured format so it fits into a table or set of related tables.

The problem is that the natural language input that apps receive from users is *unstructured*, meaning it has no predefined organizational schema. Typical examples of unstructured data include text and multimedia content, such as emails, web pages, business documents, videos, photos, and so on. Although you can still store unstructured data in a database, usually you must perform some preprocessing when you insert it. For example, you might need to label photos so the database can classify them or assign IDs to text documents so the database can distinguish between them.

Sometimes, you might need to perform more radical transformations to unstructured text content, such as extracting pieces of information from it, before grouping those pieces into a formatted structure. For example, a business chatbot typically needs to parse a customer's utterances to fill in a certain form. A different app might extract just certain elements from a web page, label those elements, and then convert the information into a table, as shown in Figure 9-1.

Unstructured data

Apelsin is a software development company based in San Francisco. The company is quite small, with only 26 employees, generating annual revenue of approximately $2 million.

Structured data

Company	Activity	Location	Staff	Revenue
Apelsin	Software development	San Francisco	26	2,000,000

Figure 9-1: An example of converting unstructured content into structured data

Tools like spaCy reveal a text's internal structure by tagging each token in a sentence with linguistic annotations. This preprocessing enables you to extract specific elements from it, usually by checking the text's syntactic dependency labels. Figure 9-2 describes how a food-ordering chatbot might recognize and extract necessary elements from a user's utterance by relying on the syntactic dependency labels spaCy assigns to each token when you apply the text-processing pipeline to it.

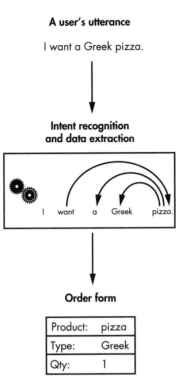

A user's utterance

I want a Greek pizza.

Intent recognition and data extraction

I want a Greek pizza.

Order form

Product:	pizza
Type:	Greek
Qty:	1

Figure 9-2: A high-level view of how raw
text can be converted into row–column data.

Next, you'll see how, once you've extracted these elements, you can
structure and insert them into a database table as a row.

Extracting Data into Interchange Formats

Many current relational databases natively support multiple common data
interchange formats. For example, MySQL natively supports XML and
JSON, the two most common data interchange formats on the web.

Your data format choice can affect the way in which you decide to collect data. For example, if the database you're using supports JSON, you can
extract data directly into a JSON object that you'll then send to the database for further processing. A JSON object is a key-value data format sur-
rounded by curly brackets. It looks like this:

```
{"product": "pizza", "type": "Chicago", "qty": 1}
```

Apart from basic values, such as strings and numbers, JSON supports
complex values, such as arrays and other JSON objects. You'll see how this
works in "Building a Database-Powered Chatbot" on page 132.

In fact, using the JSON format significantly simplifies the process of
composing a data structure for the database in your Python script. First,
you don't need to prepare a structure that conforms to a less widely used

format, which makes your code less tied to a given database type. Second, the elements in a JSON object can follow any order, which imposes fewer restrictions on how the process of determining and extraction of necessary elements from an input text can be organized.

Figure 9-3 illustrates how a food-ordering chatbot app might interact with its underlying database using JSON.

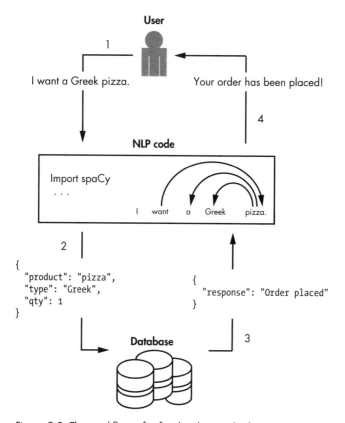

Figure 9-3: The workflow of a food-ordering chatbot app

In step 1, a user submits a request to the chatbot asking for a Greek pizza. In step 2, the chatbot processes the submitted utterance with spaCy, generating a JSON object that contains the information needed to take an order. In step 3, the JSON object representing the order form is submitted to the database, which stores the form and generates a response about it for the chatbot. In step 4, the chatbot informs the user about whether or not the order has been placed.

Moving Application Logic to the Database

Notice that the database in the chatbot application in Figure 9-3 not only stores the submitted JSON object, but also generates a response to the application about whether the operation of saving the order has been successful. The reason is that the database runs a portion of the application logic.

It's quite common for database-powered applications to keep application logic related to data processing within the database. This approach allows you to reduce data moves between the application's logic tier and the underlying database, eliminating redundancy, improving data processing efficiency, and maintaining data security.

Figure 9-4 details the database part of the chatbot application depicted in Figure 9-3.

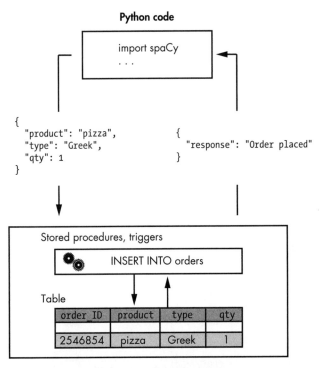

Figure 9-4: A more detailed view of the database used in the chatbot application depicted in Figure 9-3

In this application, the database will convert an input JSON object into relational data and store that data in a relational table in a way that guarantees that the data being inserted is correct and complete. If the value of a field is missing, the customer receives a message about what information they should supply.

You can check the value of each field before moving the input to the table with the help of stored procedures, ON ERROR clauses in SQL statements, or triggers defined on the table to which the data is sent. A more thorough discussion of SQL is outside the scope of this book. But in "Preparing Your Database Environment" on page 135, you'll see an example of using SQL to create a database infrastructure to be used in the application, and then interact with this infrastructure using Python.

If you're using a database that doesn't support features like converting JSON data into relational data, you'll need to implement the logic that checks the data for completeness in Python on your own; however, this discussion is beyond the scope of this chapter.

Building a Database-Powered Chatbot

Now that you have a basic idea of how to implement a database-powered chatbot app, let's create a simple one for the application shown in Figure 9-3. The app should process a user's utterance, extracting the information necessary to fill in an order form, such as product name, product type, and amount. Then this information gets packed into a JSON object that is sent to the underlying database. The database should shred the JSON object into relational data and then send a response to the application based on the data's completeness.

Gathering the Data and Building a JSON Object

We'll start by developing the application's logic tier and use Python to build a JSON object that we could then send to any database type. The following code shows what this implementation might look like:

```
  import spacy
  nlp = spacy.load('en')
  doc = nlp(u'I want a Greek pizza.')
❶ orderdict ={}
❷ for token in doc:
❸   if token.dep_ == 'dobj':
      dobj = token
❹     orderdict.update(product = dobj.lemma_)
❺     for child in dobj.lefts:
❻       if child.dep_ == 'amod' or child.dep_ == 'compound':
          orderdict.update(ptype = child.text )
❼       elif child.dep_ == 'det':
          orderdict.update(qty = 1 )
❽       elif child.dep_ == 'nummod':
          orderdict.update(qty = child.text)
        break
```

We define the `orderdict` dictionary as a container for the JSON object being created ❶. We'll be able to easily convert this dictionary to a JSON string later.

Then we iterate over the utterance's tokens ❷, looking for a direct object ❸. We might want a pizza, or we might ask someone to make us a pizza. In either case, "pizza" will be a direct object in our utterance so we're hunting for a direct object here. Of course, a real implementation would make more checks.

Once it's found, we define a key-value pair in the `orderdict` dictionary, sending in `product` as the key and the direct object's lemma as the value ❹.

We use lemmatization to reduce the possible word forms of a product's name to its base form (converting from plural to singular in most cases).

Next, we iterate over the direct object's syntactic left children ❺, because that's where we expect the information about the type of product requested. In terms of syntactic dependency labels, the product type can be either a compound or an adjectival modifier (amod) ❻. For example, spaCy would consider the word "Greek" in the phrase "a Greek pizza" an adjectival modifier, whereas it considers the word "Chicago" in the phrase "a Chicago pizza" a compound.

Now we check for the presence of a determiner in the children of the modifier or compound. The presence of the "a" determiner implies that a customer requests a single unit of a product ❼. In contrast, a word labeled with the dependency label nummod would indicate a particular number of units ❽.

Print the orderdict dictionary using this command:

```
print(orderdict)
```

This should give you the following result:

```
{'product': 'pizza', 'ptype': 'Greek', 'qty': 1}
```

Now we have a JSON string that we can send to an underlying database for further processing.

Converting Number Words to Numbers

Before moving on to the code that will send your JSON string to a database, consider what it will look like when a user explicitly specifies the quantity of a product, as in the following utterance:

```
I want two Greek pizzas.
```

If you put this into the previous script, you'd get the following result:

```
{'product': 'pizza', 'ptype': 'Greek', 'qty': two}
```

In the first sample sentence, the value of the 'qty' key is a numeral. In the second, it's a number spelled out as a word. At this stage, this difference doesn't look like a problem. But the issue is that we must define a data type for each column of a relational table when we create it. Attempting to insert data of another type into that column will fail.

You should prepare your chatbot for the fact that customers will specify a product's quantity in any way they like. To solve this problem, you'll have to convert strings representing number words to their corresponding integer values.

To do this, define a list containing numbers spelled in words and sorted in increasing order; then iterate over that list to find the correct number.

In this example, we define a list for number words ranging from "zero" to "twenty," which assumes we don't expect that a customer will order more than twenty units of the same product with one transaction.

We need to implement this conversion scenario as a function that takes either a number word or a number (in the latter case, no conversion is needed) and returns a number. We should then use the function to modify the script's code in the preceding section. Here is what the implementation of such a function might look like:

```
❶ def word2int(numword):
     num = 0
❷ try:
   ❸ num = int(numword)
   ❹ return num
     except ValueError:
   ❺ pass
❻ words = ["zero", "one", "two", "three", "four", "five", "six", "seven",
     "eight","nine", "ten", "eleven", "twelve", "thirteen", "fourteen",
     "fifteen", "sixteen", "seventeen", "eighteen", "nineteen", "twenty"]
❼ for idx, word in enumerate(words):
     ❽ if word in numword:
            num = idx
❾ return num
```

The word2int() function takes a single parameter: either a number word to be converted to the correspondent digits or a number already, in which case we won't need to convert it ❶. The function has to handle both cases, because we don't know which one we'll find in a customer's utterance.

We use the try and except block to handle cases when no conversion is needed ❷. We check whether the input is an integer ❸, and if it is, all we have to do is return the input number as is ❹. Otherwise, we ignore an error caused by an attempt to treat a nonnumber value as an integer and move on to converting it to a number ❺.

We define a list of number words, starting from zero and listing them in increasing order ❻. Then we iterate over this list with the enumerate() method ❼, looking for the word the function received as input ❽. When we find the match, we return the iteration number (the index of the word in the list) as the digit representation of the input number word ❾.

Add the word2int() function definition to the previous script. Then move to the end of the script and find the following lines of code:

```
elif child.dep_ == 'nummod':
    orderdict.update(qty = child.text)
```

Change them as follows, using the word2int() function defined in this section:

```
elif child.dep_ == 'nummod':
    orderdict.update(qty = word2int(child.text))
```

Now let's see how the script handles this sentence:

```
I want two Greek pizzas.
```

This time, you should get the following result:

```
{'product': 'pizza', 'ptype': 'Greek', 'qty': 2}
```

The value of the 'qty' field is now a digit, and we have a consistent format to send to the database.

Preparing Your Database Environment

To prepare your database environment, you need to install or obtain access to a database; create the components you'll need in the database, such as a database schema, a table, and so on; and install a Python module that enables you to interact with the database.

Although you can choose any database that can receive and process JSON data, such as an Oracle database, this section uses MySQL. The MySQL database has a long history of supporting the most popular data interchange formats, which are XML and JSON. Also, MySQL is the world's most popular open source database and is available on a majority of modern operating systems, including Linux, Windows, Unix, and macOS. MySQL has a freely downloadable version and commercial editions to meet specific business requirements.

For this chapter, you can use MySQL Community Edition—the freely downloadable version available under the GPL license. To learn more about the MySQL Community Edition, visit its official page at *https://www.mysql.com /products/community/*.

You'll first need to install MySQL on your system. At the time of this writing, MySQL 8.0 is the most recent version. Refer to the "Installing and Upgrading MySQL" chapter at *https://dev.mysql.com/doc/refman/8.0/en /installing.html* in the MySQL 8.0 Reference Manual, or the equivalent chapter for future versions of MySQL. Here, you'll find the detailed installation instructions for your operating system.

After installation, you can start the MySQL server using the command the installation guide specifies for your operating system. Before you can start working with the database, you need to obtain a password for the mysql superuser ('root'@'localhost') generated during the installation. You'll find the password in the installation error log file.

Once you have the superuser password, you can connect to the MySQL server from a system terminal using the following command:

```
$ mysql -uroot -p
Enter password: ******
mysql>
```

If you prefer to use a GUI, you can take advantage of MySQL Workbench (*https://www.mysql.com/products/workbench/*), which is a unified visual tool designed to model and manage MySQL databases.

After connecting to the server, your first step is to choose a new password for the root user, replacing the random password generated during the installation. Use the following command to do so:

```
ALTER USER 'root'@'localhost' IDENTIFIED BY 'Your-pswd';
```

Now you're ready to start developing the infrastructure on the server that you need for your application. You'll begin by creating a database that you'll use as the container for the other objects the application needs to interact with. To create the database, enter the following command at the mysql> prompt:

```
mysql> CREATE DATABASE mybot;
Query OK, 1 row affected (0.03 sec)
```

Then select the newly created database for use, as follows:

```
mysql> USE mybot;
Database changed
```

You're ready to start creating your database's structure. For this example, you'll need a single table you create with the following command:

```
CREATE TABLE orders (
  id INT NOT NULL AUTO_INCREMENT,
  product VARCHAR(30),
  ptype VARCHAR(30),
  qty INT,
  PRIMARY KEY (id)
);
```

With this database infrastructure set up, you need to install the MySQL Connector/Python driver, which allows your Python code to interact with that infrastructure. On any operating system, you can install Connector/Python via pip, as follows:

```
pip install mysql-connector-python
```

For further details on how to install this driver, check the documentation at *https://dev.mysql.com/doc/connector-python/en/*.

Using the following simple script, ensure that you've installed Connector/Python:

```
import mysql.connector
cnx = mysql.connector.connect(user='root', password='Your_pswd',
                              host='127.0.0.1',
                              database='mybot')
cnx.close()
```

If the install is successful, you should see no error messages.

Sending Data to the Underlying Database

Let's return to the script we had on page 134. The following code connects to your database and passes order data to the orders table. Append this code to the script:

```
   import json
❶ json_str = json.dumps(orderdict)
   import mysql.connector
   from mysql.connector import errorcode
   try:
❷   cnx = mysql.connector.connect(user='root', password='Your_pswd',
                                     host='127.0.0.1',
                                     database='mybot')
❸   query = ("""INSERT INTO orders (product, ptype, qty)
      SELECT product, ptype, qty FROM
          JSON_TABLE(
❹         %s,
            "$" COLUMNS(
              qty     INT PATH '$.qty',
              product VARCHAR(30) PATH "$.product",
              ptype   VARCHAR(30) PATH "$.ptype"
            )
          ) AS jt1""")
❺   cursor = cnx.cursor()
❻   cursor.execute(query, ❼(json_str,))
❽   cnx.commit()
❾ except mysql.connector.Error as err:
      print("Error-Code:", err.errno)
      print("Error-Message: {}".format(err.msg))
   finally:
      cursor.close()
      cnx.close()
```

We start by converting the orderdict dictionary into a JSON string ❶. Next, we connect to the database ❷ and define an insert SQL statement to be passed into the database for processing ❸. Note the use of a placeholder (called a *bind variable*) in the statement ❹. Using placeholders allows us to write SQL statements that accept inputs at runtime.

Before we can execute the statement, we create a mysql.connector cursor object ❺, which enables operations over the objects in the database we're connected to. Then we can execute the INSERT statement ❻, binding the JSON string ❼ we obtained in the beginning of this code snippet to the placeholder in the statement. Note the use of the JSON_TABLE function that shreds the submitted JSON data to tabular data, making it appropriate for inserting into a relational table.

After the execution of the INSERT statement, we need to explicitly commit the statement's changes with the commit() method ❽. Otherwise, the insertion will roll back when the connection closes (either explicitly with cnx.close() or when the script's execution is complete).

The except block will begin to execute if an error occurs on the database side ❾. In the next section, you'll learn how to take advantage of this functionality when the JSON string passed in doesn't contain all the fields.

Now execute the script. If you don't see any error messages, return to the mysql prompt you worked with in the preceding section and enter the following select statement:

```
mysql> SELECT * FROM orders;

ID    PRODUCT      PTYPE     QTY
----  -----------  --------  ---
1     pizza        Greek     2
```

If you can see this output, your Python script is working as expected.

When a User's Request Doesn't Contain Enough Information

Sometimes, a user's request might not contain enough information to fill in all the fields in the order form. As an example, consider the following utterance:

```
I want two pizzas.
```

Table 9-1 shows the order form the application discussed here will generate from this sentence.

Table 9-1: An Order Form Missing Information

product	ptype	quantity
pizza		2

The value of the ptype field is missing because the user didn't identify the type of pizza they want. To address this issue, enhance the INSERT statement in the previous script as follows:

```
query = ("""INSERT INTO orders (product, ptype, qty)
SELECT product, ptype, qty FROM
    JSON_TABLE(
        %s,
        "$"
        COLUMNS(
            qty      INT PATH '$.qty' ❶ERROR ON EMPTY,
            product  VARCHAR(30) PATH "$.product" ❶ERROR ON EMPTY,
            ptype    VARCHAR(30) PATH "$.ptype" ❶ERROR ON EMPTY
        )
    ) AS jt1""");
```

We add the ERROR ON EMPTY option ❶ to each column in JSON_TABLE. This option allows us to handle errors caused by trying to insert a JSON string that doesn't contain all the fields it's supposed to contain.

Now when you execute the script with the "I want two pizzas." sample sentence, you should see the following output:

```
Error-Code: 3665
Error-Message: Missing value for JSON_TABLE column 'ptype'
```

We could expand on the script so in such cases the chatbot asks the customer to clarify their order using the following question:

```
What type of pizza do you want?
```

An answer might look like this:

```
I want Greek ones.
```

The structure of the sentence representing the answer we're supposed to receive here is similar to the structure of the original sentence. Therefore, we can use the same code to analyze this answer that we used to analyze the original sentence. Of course, this approach makes assumptions about a user's response. A real implementation would start with this approach and then, if necessary, move on to the other possible response structures. For example, a user's response might consist of a single word, "Greek." In that case, all we need to do is to check whether it's included in our list of pizza types.

Try This

The error message tells you what specific field is missing. But you still need to extract this field name from the message so you can ask the customer to clarify a specific part of their order. One way to do this is to look at the object of the preposition in the message. For example, in the message, `Error-Message: Missing value for JSON_TABLE column 'ptype'`, the object of the preposition is `ptype`.

Summary

In this chapter, you learned how to cut raw text into shreds to insert the text into a relational database. You used the JSON format to interact with a database that can process a JSON input, extracting it into relational data. You also learned to implement some application logic within the database with the help of pure SQL, allowing you to move data processing closer to the data. To implement more complicated scenarios, you might need to use triggers and stored procedures—the details can be found in the documentation for the database you're using.

10

TRAINING MODELS

As you learned in Chapter 1, spaCy contains statistical neural network models trained to perform named entity recognition, part-of-speech tagging, syntactic dependency parsing, and semantic similarity prediction. But you're not limited to using only pretrained, ready-to-use models. You can also train a model with your own training examples, tuning its pipeline components for your application's requirements.

This chapter covers how to train spaCy's named entity recognizer and dependency parser, the pipeline components that you most often need to customize to make the model you're using specific to a particular use case. The reason is that a certain domain usually requires a specific set of entities and, sometimes, a certain way of parsing dependencies. You'll learn how to train an existing model with new examples and a blank one from scratch. You'll also save a customized pipeline component to disk so you can load it later in another script or model.

Training a Model's Pipeline Component

You rarely have to train a model from scratch to satisfy your application's specific requirements. Instead, you can use an existing model and update only the pipeline component you need to change. This process usually involves two steps: preparing *training examples* (sets of sentences with annotations that the model can learn from), and then exposing the pipeline component to the training examples, as shown in Figure 10-1.

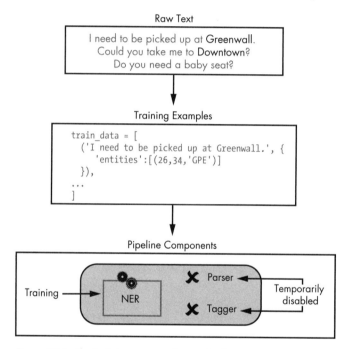

Figure 10-1: The training process for a pipeline component

To prepare training examples, you convert raw text data into a training example containing a sentence and each token's annotations. During the training process, spaCy uses the training examples to correct the model's weights: the goal is to minimize the error (called the *loss*) of the model prediction. Put simply, the algorithm calculates the relationship between the token and its annotation to determine the likelihood that a token should be assigned that annotation.

A real-world implementation might require hundreds or even thousands of training examples to efficiently teach a certain component of a model. Before you start training the component, you need to temporarily disable all the model's other pipeline components to protect them from unnecessary alterations.

Training the Entity Recognizer

Suppose you're developing a chatbot app for a taxi company. The app must correctly recognize all the names referring to districts within the city and its surroundings. To accomplish this, you might need to update a model's named entity recognition system with your own examples, making it recognize, for instance, the word "Solnce," which refers to a neighborhood in a city, as a geopolitical entity. The following sections describe how you could complete this task.

Deciding Whether You Need to Train the Entity Recognizer

Let's begin by looking at how the existing named entity recognizer in the default English model (generally the en_core_web_sm model) recognizes the named entities of interest. It's possible that you won't need to update the named entity recognizer. For this task, you might use sentences common for booking a taxi, like this one:

```
Could you pick me up at Solnce?
```

To see how the recognizer will classify "Solnce" in the sentence, print the sentence's named entities using the following script:

```
import spacy
nlp = spacy.load('en')
doc = nlp(u'Could you pick me up at Solnce?')
  for ent in doc.ents:
    print(ent.text, ent.label_)
```

In this example, "Solnce" is the only named entity, so the script generates the following single-line output:

```
Solnce LOC
```

Note that the output for this entity can vary depending on the model and sentence you're using. To get the description for the LOC entity label in the output, you can use the spacy.explain() function:

```
>>> print(spacy.explain('LOC'))
'Non-GPE locations, mountain ranges, bodies of water'
```

The result is that the named entity recognizer classified "Solnce" as a non-GPE location, which doesn't match what you expect to see. To change this so the recognizer classifies "Solnce" as an entity of type GPE, you need to update the recognizer, as discussed in the following sections.

NOTE *For simplicity, we're using a single-named entity in this example. But you can create more names for districts with which to train the recognizer.*

Rather than updating the existing recognizer, you could replace it with a custom one. However, in that case, you'd need many more training examples to retain the functionality that isn't related to GPE entities but you might still need.

Creating Training Examples

Once you know you need to train the entity recognizer to satisfy your app's needs, the next step is to create a set of appropriate training examples. For that, you need some relevant text.

Likely, the best data source for creating such a training set is real customer input that you gathered previously. Choose utterances that include the named entities you need to use for training. Typically, you'd log customer input in a file as plaintext. For example, a customer input log file for the taxi app might contain the following utterances:

```
Could you send a taxi to Solnce?
Is there a flat rate to the airport from Solnce?
How long is the wait for a taxi right now?
```

To create training examples from these utterances, you need to convert them into a list of tuples in which each training example represents a separate tuple, as shown here:

```
train_exams = [
❶ ('Could you send a taxi to Solnce?', {
      ❷ 'entities': [(25, 32, 'GPE')]
    }),
    ('Is there a flat rate to the airport from Solnce?', {
        'entities': [(41, 48, 'GPE')]
    }),
    ('How long is the wait for a taxi right now?', {
        'entities': []
    })
]
```

Each tuple consists of two values: the string representing an utterance ❶ and the dictionary for the annotations of the entities found in that utterance. The entity's annotations include its start and end positions in terms of characters composing the utterance and the label to be assigned to the entity ❷.

Automating the Example Creation Process

As you've no doubt realized, creating a set of training examples manually can be time-consuming and error prone, especially if you have hundreds or thousands of utterances to process. You can automate this tedious task by using the following script, which quickly creates a set of training examples from the submitted text.

```
   import spacy
   nlp = spacy.load('en')
❶ doc = nlp(u'Could you send a taxi to Solnce? I need to get to Google. Could
   you send a taxi an hour later?')
❷ #f = open("test.txt","rb")
   #contents =f.read()
   #doc = nlp(contents.decode('utf8'))
❸ train_exams = []
❹ districts = ['Solnce', 'Greenwal', 'Downtown']
   for sent in doc.sents:
     entities = []
     for token in sent:
       if token.ent_type != 0:
❺        start = token.idx - sent.start_char
           if token.text in districts:
             entity = (start, start + len(token), 'GPE')
           else:
             entity = (start, start + len(token), token.ent_type_)
           entities.append(entity)
     tpl = (sent.text, {'entities': entities})
❻    train_exams.append(tpl)
```

For readability, we pick up some utterances for processing in the usual way: by hardcoding them in the script ❶. But the commented lines of code show how we might pick up utterances from a file instead ❷.

Once we've obtained the utterances—either from a file or passed in to the doc explicitly—we can start generating a list of training examples from them. We begin by creating an empty list ❸. Next, we need to define a list containing the names of entities that we want the model to recognize differently than it currently does ❹. (This is the list of districts in this example.)

Remember that real customer input might include entities that the recognizer already correctly recognizes (say, Google or London), so we shouldn't change the recognizer's behavior when it classifies them. We create training examples for those entities and process all the entities presented in the utterances used for generating training examples, not only the new ones. A training set for a real implementation must include numerous examples for entities of different types. Depending on the application's needs, the training set might include several hundred examples.

We iterate over the submitted utterances, creating a new empty entities list on each iteration. Then, to fill in this list, we loop over the tokens in the utterance, finding entities. For each found entity, we determine its start character index in the utterance ❺. We then calculate the end index by adding len(token) to the start index.

Also, we must check whether the entity is in the list of entities to which we want to assign a new label. If so, we assign it the GPE label. Otherwise, the recognizer will use the current label in the entity annotations. After that, we can define a tuple representing the training example, and then append it to the training set ❻.

The script sends the training examples being generated to the train
_exams list, which should look as follows after the script execution:

```
>>> train_exams
[
❶ ('Could you send a taxi to Solnce?', {'entities': [(25, 31, 'GPE')]}),
❷ ('I need to get to Google.', {'entities': [(17, 23, 'ORG')]}),
❸ ('Could you send a taxi an hour later?', {'entities': []})
]
```

For simplicity, the training set we use here consists of just a few training examples. Notice that only the first one contains an entity from the
list of entities we need to familiarize the recognizer with (the districts list
in this example) ❶. That doesn't mean that the second and third training
examples aren't useful. The second training example ❷ mixes in another
entity type, which prevents the recognizer from "forgetting" what it previously knew.

The third training example doesn't contain any entity ❸. To improve the
learning results, we need to mix in not only examples of other entity types,
but also examples that don't contain any entities. The following section "The
Training Process" discusses the details of the training process.

Disabling the Other Pipeline Components

The spaCy documentation recommends disabling all the other pipeline components before you start training a certain pipeline component, so you modify only the component you want to update. The following code disables all
the pipeline components except for the named entity recognizer. You need to
either append this code to the script introduced in the preceding section or
execute it in the same Python session after that script (we'll append the final
piece of code in the next section, which covers the training process):

```
other_pipes = [pipe for pipe in nlp.pipe_names if pipe != 'ner']
nlp.disable_pipes(*other_pipes)
```

Now you're ready to start training the named entity recognizer to teach
it to find the new entities defined in the training examples.

The Training Process

In the training process, you shuffle and loop over the training examples,
adjusting the model with weights that more accurately reflect the relationships between the tokens and the annotations. Refer back to Chapter 1
for a more detailed explanation of neural network models, including what
weights are.

To improve accuracy, you can apply several techniques to a training
loop. For example, the following code illustrates how to process your training examples in batches. This technique shows the training examples to the
model in different representations to avoid generalizations found in the
training corpus.

Append the following code to the script that was first introduced in "Creating Training Examples" on page 144 and that was modified in the preceding section.

```
  import random
  from spacy.util import minibatch, compounding
❶ optimizer = nlp.entity.create_optimizer()
  for i in range(25):
  ❷ random.shuffle(train_exams)
    max_batch_size = 3
  ❸ batch_size = compounding(2.0, max_batch_size, 1.001)
  ❹ batches = minibatch(train_exams, size=batch_size)
    for batch in batches:
        texts, annotations = zip(*batch)
      ❺ nlp.update(texts, annotations, sgd=optimizer)
❻ ner = nlp.get_pipe('ner')
❼ ner.to_disk('/usr/to/ner')
```

Before we can begin training, we need to create an *optimizer* ❶—a function that will be used during the training process to hold intermediate results between updates of the model weights. We could create an optimizer with the nlp.begin_training() method. But this method removes existing entity types. In this example, because we're updating an existing model and don't want it to "forget" the existing entity types, we use the nlp.entity.create _optimizer() method. This method creates an optimizer for the named entity recognizer without losing an existing set of entity types.

During the training process, the script shows the examples to the model in a loop, in random order, to avoid any generalizations that might come from the order of the examples ❷. The script also batches the training examples, which the spaCy documentation suggests might improve the effectiveness of the training process when the number of training examples is large enough. To make the batch size vary on each step, we use the compounding() method, which yields a generator of batch sizes. In particular, it generates an infinite series of compounding values: it starts from the value specified as the first parameter and calculates the next value by multiplying the previous value by the compound rate specified as the third parameter, without exceeding the maximum value specified as the second parameter ❸. Then we batch the training examples using the minibatch() method. Doing so sets its size parameter to the iterator generated with the compounding() method invoked in the preceding line of code ❹.

Next, we iterate over the batches, updating the named entity recognizer model on each iteration. Each batch requires us to update the model by calling nlp.update() ❺, which makes a prediction for each entity found in the examples included in the batch and then checks the annotations provided to see whether it was correct. If the prediction is wrong, the training process adjusts the weights in the underlying model so the correct prediction will score higher next time.

Finally, we need to serialize the updated named entity recognizer component to disk so we can load it in another script (or another Python session) later. For that, we first must obtain the component from the pipeline ❻ and then save it to disk with its to_disk() method ❼. Be sure you've created the */usr/to* directory in your system.

Evaluating the Updated Recognizer

Now you can test the updated recognizer. If you're performing the example discussed in this chapter in a Python session, close it, open a new one, and enter the following code to make sure the model has made the correct generalizations. (If you've built a separate script from the code discussed in the previous sections and run it, you can run the following code either as a separate script or from within a Python session.)

```
import spacy
from spacy.pipeline import EntityRecognizer
❶ nlp = spacy.load('en', disable=['ner'])
❷ ner = EntityRecognizer(nlp.vocab)
❸ ner.from_disk('/usr/to/ner')
❹ nlp.add_pipe(ner, "custom_ner")
❺ print(nlp.meta['pipeline'])
❻ doc = nlp(u'Could you pick me up at Solnce?')
  for ent in doc.ents:
    print(ent.text, ent.label_)
```

We first load the pipeline components without the named entity recognizer component ❶. The reason is that training an existing model's pipeline component doesn't permanently override the component's original behavior. When we load a model, the original versions of the components composing the model's pipeline load by default; so to use an updated version, we must explicitly load it from disk. This allows us to have several custom versions of the same pipeline component and load an appropriate one when necessary.

We create this new component in two steps: constructing a new pipeline instance from the EntityRecognizer class ❷, and then loading the data into it from disk, specifying the directory in which we serialized the recognizer ❸.

Next, we add the loaded named entity recognizer component to the current pipeline, optionally using a custom name ❹. If we print out the names of the currently available pipeline components ❺, we should see that custom name among the 'tagger' and 'parser' names.

The only task left is test the loaded named entity recognizer component. Be sure to use a different sentence than the one used in the training dataset ❻.

As a result, we should see the following output:

```
Available pipe components: ['tagger', 'parser', 'custom_ner']
Solnce GPE
```

The updated named entity recognizer component can now recognize the custom entity names correctly.

Creating a New Dependency Parser

In the following sections, you'll learn how to create a custom dependency parser suitable for a specific task. In particular, you'll train a parser that reveals semantic relations in a sentence rather than syntactic dependencies. *Semantic relations* are between the meanings of words and phrases in a sentence.

Custom Syntactic Parsing to Understand User Input

Why would you need semantic relations? Well, suppose your chatbot app is supposed to understand a user's request, expressed in plain English, and then transform it into a SQL query to be passed into a database. To achieve this, the app performs syntactic parsing to extract the meaning, shredding the input into pieces to use in building a database query. For example, imagine you have the following sentence to parse:

```
Find a high paid job with no experience.
```

A SQL query generated from this sentence might look like this:

```
SELECT * FROM jobs WHERE salary = 'high' AND experience = 'no'
```

To begin with, let's look at how a regular dependency parser would process the sample sentence. For that, you might use the following script:

```
import spacy
nlp = spacy.load('en')
doc = nlp(u'Find a high paid job with no experience.')
print([(t.text, t.dep_, t.head.text) for t in doc])
```

The script outputs each token's text, its dependency label, and its syntactic head. If you're using the en_core_web_sm model, the result should look as follows:

```
[
  ('Find', 'ROOT', 'Find'),
  ('a', 'det', 'job'),
  ('high', 'amod', 'job'),
  ('paid', 'amod', 'job'),
  ('job', 'dobj', 'Find'),
  ('with', 'prep', 'Find'),
  ('no', 'det', 'experience'),
  ('experience', 'pobj', 'with'),
  ('.', 'punct', 'Find')
]
```

Diagrammatically, this dependency parsing looks like Figure 10-2.

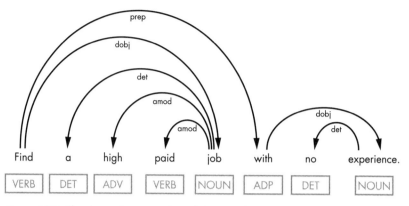

Figure 10-2: The dependency parsing of the sample sentence

This syntactic parsing probably won't help you generate the desired database query from the sentence. The SQL query shown earlier in this section uses the SELECT statement to select a job that satisfies the requirements "high paid" and "no experience." In this logic, the word "job" should be connected with not only "high paid" but also "no experience," but the syntactic parsing doesn't connect "job" with "no experience."

To meet your processing needs, you might want to change labeling in a way that will simplify the task of generating database queries. For that, you need to implement a custom parser that shows semantic relations rather than syntactic dependencies. In this case, that means you'd want an arc between the words "job" and "experience." The following sections describe how to implement this.

Deciding on Types of Semantic Relations to Use

First, you need to choose a set of relation types to use for labeling. The spaCy documentation contains an example of a custom message parser (*https://spacy.io/usage/training/#intent-parser*) that uses the following semantic relations: ROOT, PLACE, ATTRIBUTE, QUALITY, TIME, and LOCATION. You might, for example, assign PLACE to a place at which some activity occurs, like "hotel" in the utterance, "I need a hotel in Berlin." "Berlin" would be a LOCATION in this same utterance, allowing you to distinguish between geographical areas and smaller settings.

To comply with the semantics used in this example, you might add one more type to the list: ACTIVITY, which you could use to label the word "job" in the sample sentence. (Of course, you could just use the original set of relation types. After all, a job is typically associated with a workplace, for which you could use the type PLACE.)

Creating Training Examples

As usual for the process of training a pipeline component, you start by preparing training examples. When training a parser, you need information about each token's dependency label and the head of each relation. In this example, you use only a couple of training examples to keep it short and simple. Of course, a real-world implementation would require many more to train a parser component.

```
TRAINING_DATA = [
    ('find a high paying job with no experience', {
        'heads': [0, 4, 4, 4, 0, 7, 7, 4],
        'deps': ['ROOT', '-', 'QUALITY', 'QUALITY', 'ACTIVITY', '-', 'QUALITY', 'ATTRIBUTE']
    }),
    ('find good workout classes near home', {
        'heads': [0, 4, 4, 4, 0, 6, 4],
        'deps': ['ROOT', '-', 'QUALITY', 'QUALITY', 'ACTIVITY', 'QUALITY', 'ATTRIBUTE']
    })
]
```

Notice that the syntactically related words might not always be related semantically in the new parser. To see this clearly, you can perform the following test, which generates a list of the heads of the *syntactic* dependencies found in the sample sentence from the first training example in the TRAINING_DATA list:

```
import spacy
nlp = spacy.load('en')
doc = nlp(u'find a high paying job with no experience')
heads = []
for token in doc:
    heads.append(token.head.i)
print(heads)
```

Assuming you're using the en_core_web_sm model, this code should output the following token head indexes:

```
[0, 4, 4, 4, 0, 4, 7, 5]
```

When you compare this list with the heads provided for this same sentence in the TRAINING_DATA list, you should notice discrepancies. For example, in the training example, the word "with" is a child of the word "experience," whereas, according to standard syntactic rules, "with" is a child of "job" in this sentence. This deviation makes sense if we slightly change the sentence:

```
find a high paying job without any experience
```

In terms of semantics, "without" can be thought of as a modifier for "experience," because "without" changes the meaning of "experience." Modifiers, in turn, are always dependent on the word they modify. Therefore, considering "without" as the child in the without/experience pair in this example is quite reasonable when taking semantics into consideration.

Training the Parser

The following script illustrates how to train a parser from scratch using a blank model. In this example, creating a brand-new parser is more reasonable than updating an existing one: the reason is that attempting to train an existing syntactic dependency parser to recognize semantic relations as well would be very difficult, because the two kinds of relations often conflict. But this doesn't mean that you can't use your custom parser with existing models. You can load it to any model to replace its original syntactic dependency parser.

To train the parser, the following script uses the training examples from the TRAINING_DATA list defined in the preceding section. Be sure to prepend the TRAINING_DATA list to the code that follows:

```
import spacy
❶ nlp = spacy.blank('en')
❷ parser = nlp.create_pipe('parser')
❸ nlp.add_pipe(parser, first=True)
❹ for text, annotations in TRAINING_DATA:
    ❺ for d in annotations.get('deps', []):
        ❻ parser.add_label(d)
❼ optimizer = nlp.begin_training()
   import random
❽ for i in range(25):
    ❾ random.shuffle(TRAINING_DATA)
       for text, annotations in TRAINING_DATA:
           nlp.update([text], [annotations], sgd=optimizer)
❿ parser.to_disk('/home/oracle/to/parser')
```

We start by creating a blank model ❶. Then we create a blank parser component ❷ and add it to the model's pipeline ❸.

In this example, we derive the set of labels for the parser to use from the TRAINING_DATA list that we had to add to the code. We implement this operation in two loops. In the outer loop, we iterate over the training examples, extracting the tuple with the head and dependency annotations from each example ❹. In the inner loop, we iterate over the tuple of annotations, extracting each label from the deps list ❺ and adding it to the parser ❻.

Now we can start the training process. First, we acquire an optimizer ❼ and then implement a simple training loop ❽, shuffling the training examples in a random order ❾. Next, we iterate over the training examples, updating the parser model on each iteration.

Finally, we serialize the custom parser to disk so we can load and use it later in another script ❿.

Testing Your Custom Parser

You can load a custom parser from disk to an existing model's pipeline using the following script:

```
import spacy
from spacy.pipeline import DependencyParser
```

```
❶ nlp = spacy.load('en', disable=['parser'])
❷ parser = DependencyParser(nlp.vocab)
❸ parser.from_disk('/home/oracle/to/parser')
❹ nlp.add_pipe(parser, "custom_parser")
  print(nlp.meta['pipeline'])
  doc = nlp(u'find a high paid job with no degree')
❺ print([(w.text, w.dep_, w.head.text) for w in doc if w.dep_ != '-'])
```

Notice that this script is similar to the script for loading a custom named entity recognizer shown earlier in "Evaluating the Updated Recognizer" on page 148. We load a regular model, disabling a certain component—the parser, in this example ❶. Next, we create a parser ❷ and load it with the data previously serialized to disk ❸. To make the parser available, we need to add it to the model's pipeline ❹. Then we can test it ❺.

The script should produce the following output:

```
['tagger', 'ner', 'custom_parser']
[
  ('find', 'ROOT', 'find'),
  ('high', 'QUALITY', 'job'),
  ('paid', 'QUALITY', 'job'),
  ('job', 'ACTIVITY', 'find'),
  ('no', 'QUALITY', 'degree'),
  ('degree', 'ATTRIBUTE', 'job')
]
```

The original parser component has been replaced with the custom one in a regular model, whereas the other pipeline components remain the same. Later, we could reload the original component by loading the model using spacy.load('en').

Try This

Now that you have a custom parser trained to reveal semantic relations, you can put it to use. Continue with the example from this section by writing a script that generates a SQL statement from a plain English request. In that script, check the ROOT element of each request to determine whether you need to construct a SELECT statement. Then use the ACTIVITY element to refer to the database table against which the statement being generated will be executed. Use the QUALITY and ATTRIBUTE elements in the statement's WHERE clause.

Summary

You can download a set of pretrained statistical models from spaCy to use immediately. But these models might not always suit your purposes. You might want to improve a pipeline component in an existing model or create a new component in a blank model that will better suit your app's needs.

In this chapter, you learned how to train an existing named entity recognizer component to recognize an additional set of entities that weren't labeled correctly by default. Then you learned how to train a custom parser component to predict a type of tree structure related to input text that shows semantic relations rather than syntactic dependencies.

In both cases, the first (and perhaps the most important and time-consuming) step is to prepare training data. Once you've done that, you'll need only a few more lines of code to implement a training loop for your custom component.

11

DEPLOYING YOUR OWN CHATBOT

In previous chapters, you hardcoded all the input to your NLP scripts by manually assigning text to a doc object. But when you build chatbots for tasks like taking orders, things get more complicated. You'll need to deploy your app to a *bot channel*, such as Telegram, which facilitates communication between a bot and a user.

This chapter begins with an overview of how to organize a chatbot app. You'll be guided through the process of preparing a platform for your chatbot with Telegram and then deploying the bot to that platform. You'll learn how to process multiple kinds of user input with the Telegram API and hold the state of a conversation to keep track of which questions have already been asked.

How Implementing and Deploying a Chatbot Works

This section looks closely at how information is transmitted between a typical chatbot and a user, as well as at the structure this transmission needs.

A typical chatbot app consists of multiple tiers. After you've implemented the logic for processing user input on your machine, you'll need a messenger app that allows you to create accounts that programs operate. Users won't interact with the bot implementation on your machine directly; instead, they'll chat with the bot through the messenger. Apart from a messenger, your chatbot might require some additional services, such as a database or other storage.

The diagram in Figure 11-1 represents how a typical chatbot application combines these tiers.

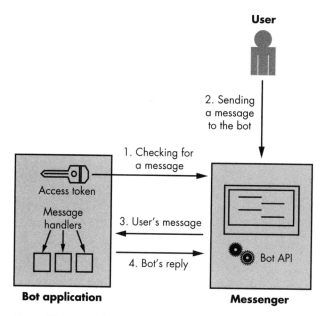

Figure 11-1: Typical interactions between a user and a bot integrated to a messenger

The bot application first sends requests to the messenger in an infinite loop, checking whether a user has started a conversation. These requests include an authentication token generated when the developer created the bot in the messenger. An *authentication token* (also called an access token or API key) is unique to the bot that allows the messenger to recognize requests coming from this particular bot.

When a user sends a message to the bot, the messenger processes it and then forwards it to the addressee. The bot chooses an appropriate *handler*—a routine that generates responses to a certain type of user messages—and sends the generated reply to the user.

The intermediary program that the chatbot uses to interact with users is often a bot platform provided by a messenger app, such as Skype, Facebook Messenger, or Telegram. From the messenger's standpoint, the bot is a third-party application that runs inside the messenger.

The next section guides you through the process of deploying a chatbot implemented in Python to the Telegram's bot platform. You'll see some bot implementation details that are specific to the Telegram's bot platform and will learn to use its features to make bot development easy.

I chose the Telegram bot platform for this example because it provides comprehensive resources for Python developers, including the Python Telegram Bot documentation, guides and tutorials, and examples on GitHub. That is, Telegram provides everything you need to build a chatbot in Python. In other messaging apps, like Facebook Messenger for example, you'd need to use third-party tools, such as Flask or Ngrok, complicating a bot's implementation and not strictly focusing on NLP tasks.

Using Telegram as a Platform for Your Bot

Telegram is a cloud-based messenger and one of the top messenger apps in the world. Among other features, it provides a platform for creating bots along with a Python library that offers an easy-to-use interface. You can use Telegram on Android, iOS, Windows, Linux, and macOS platforms. But it's primarily designed for smartphones.

Creating a Telegram Account and Authorizing Your Bot

Before you can create a bot in Telegram, you must sign up for a Telegram account. To do so, you'll need a smartphone or tablet that runs either iOS or Android. A PC version of Telegram won't work for this operation. However, once you create a Telegram account, you can use it on a PC.

You'll find steps that guide you through the process of creating a Telegram account at *https://telegramguide.com/create-a-telegram-account/*. Once you have a Telegram account, you can create a bot. You can do this from either a smartphone or a PC, as described in the following steps:

1. In the Telegram app, perform a search for @BotFather or open the URL *https://telegram.me/botfather/*. BotFather is a Telegram bot that manages all the other bots in your account.

2. On the BotFather page, click the **Start** button to see the list of commands that you can use to set up your Telegram bots.

3. To create a new bot, enter the /newbot command in the **Write a message** box. You'll be prompted for a name and a username for your bot. Then you'll be given an authorization token for the new bot. Figure 11-2 shows a screenshot of this process on a smartphone.

Figure 11-2: Creating a new bot in Telegram using a smartphone

Now you can integrate the bot functionality implemented on your machine in a Python file with the bot you just created in Telegram, as discussed in the next section.

It's important to know that a bot you just created in Telegram doesn't implement the logic for handling user input. In fact, it's just a wrapper for the actual bot you need to implement on your own.

Getting Started with the python-telegram-bot Library

To connect chatbot functionality implemented in Python, you'll need the `python-telegram-bot` library, which is built on top of the Telegram Bot API. The library provides an easy-to-use interface for bot programmers developing apps for Telegram. It allows you to focus on coding the bot rather than on the details related to the interactions between the messenger and the bot implementation.

The `python-telegram-bot` library is free software distributed under an LGPLv3 license. You can install or upgrade it via `pip` using the following command:

```
$ pip install python-telegram-bot --upgrade
```

The examples provided throughout the rest of this chapter assume that you're using `python-telegram-bot` version 12.0 or later.

Once you've installed the library, use the following lines of code to perform a quick test to verify that you can access your Telegram bot from Python. You must have an internet connection for this test to work.

```
import telegram
bot = telegram.Bot(token='XXXXXX...')
```

In place of 'XXXXX', include the token you were given when creating the bot. Then check your credentials using this line:

```
print(bot.get_me())
```

If the bot.get_me() function returns your credentials, the bot's authentication token you specified previously is valid.

Using the telegram.ext Objects

To build a real bot, you'll need to use the telegram.ext objects, including telegram.ext.Updater and telegram.ext.Dispatcher. These are two of the most important objects in the library, because they're required in every implementation. In a nutshell, an Updater object receives the messages from Telegram and delivers them to a Dispatcher. In turn, the Dispatcher passes the data to an appropriate handler for processing. The following code illustrates how to use these objects in a simple echo bot that replies to each message with a message that has the same text:

```
from telegram.ext import Updater, MessageHandler, Filters
#function that implements the message handler
❶ def echo(update, context):
    update.message.reply_text(update.message.text)
#creating an Updater instance
❷ updater = Updater('TOKEN', use_context=True)
#registering a handler to handle input text messages
updater.dispatcher.add_handler(MessageHandler(Filters.text, echo))
#starting polling updates from the messenger
updater.start_polling()
updater.idle()
```

We start by importing the Updater and MessageHandler modules from the telegram.ext package. Then we define the echo() function, which takes two objects as parameters: update and context ❶. The update object represents an incoming message, which can be text, a photo, a sticker, and so on. The context object contains attributes that can hold data from the same chat and user. Both update and context are generated for you behind the scenes and passed to the *callback*—a message processing function assigned to a certain handler. In this example, the text message handler's callback function is echo(); it contains a single line of code that instructs Telegram to return a user's text message without any change.

Next, we create an Updater object ❷, which we'll use to orchestrate the bot execution process throughout the script. When we create an Updater object, a Dispatcher object is created automatically for us, allowing us to register handlers for different types of input data, such as text and photo. In this example, we register a single handler designed to handle only text messages, passing it the callback function implemented earlier in this script. Now the chatbot will call the callback function every time it receives a Telegram message that contains text.

Then we start the bot by invoking the start_polling() method of the Updater, which launches the process of polling new messages from the messenger. Because start_polling() is a non-blocking method, we also have to call the idle() method of the Updater, which blocks our script until a message is received or a user enters an exit shortcut (CTRL-C). For further details on the classes and methods available in the python-telegram-bot library, read the Python Telegram Bot's documentation.

To test the script, run it on an internet-connected machine. Once it's running, any Telegram user can start a conversation with your chatbot. In the Telegram app, search for @*<username>*, entering the username you gave your bot when you created it; then select it. To start a conversation, click the **/start** button or enter the /start command. You can then start sending messages to your bot. Because you've implemented an echo bot, any reply message from the bot should contain the same text you sent it.

Creating a Telegram Chatbot That Uses spaCy

In the preceding section, we used the python-telegram-bot library and built a simple script integrated into Telegram. Let's now enhance our implementation and add spaCy to make sure the bot created in Telegram is fully operational.

The following code creates a simple bot that processes a user's utterance and determines whether or not it contains a direct object. Based on that information, it generates a reply message for the user. This code isn't very useful on its own, but it should show you how to connect text-processing code implemented with spaCy to the code implemented with the python-telegram-bot library.

```
import spacy
from telegram.ext import Updater, MessageHandler, Filters
#the callback function that uses spaCy
❶ def utterance(update, context):
  msg = update.message.text
  nlp = spacy.load('en')
  doc = nlp(msg)
  for token in doc:
    if token.dep_ == 'dobj':
      update.message.reply_text('We are processing your request...')
      return
  update.message.reply_text('Please rephrase your request. Be as specific as
  possible!')
#the code responsible for interactions with Telegram
updater = Updater('TOKEN', use_context=True)
updater.dispatcher.add_handler(MessageHandler(Filters.text, utterance))
updater.start_polling()
updater.idle()
```

Notice that the code responsible for interactions with Telegram is the same as in the preceding script. The only difference here is the implementation of the callback function ❶. In this case, the utterance() function uses spaCy to process a user's input.

In that function, we first extract the message text from the update object passed to the function. Next, we convert it into a spaCy Doc object and then check whether the utterance in the doc includes a direct object. If the utterance doesn't include a direct object, we ask the user to be more specific. For example, a user might say "I am hungry," which implies they want to order some food. But to place an order, we need them to be more specific; for example, "I want a pizza."

Perhaps the most interesting aspect of this example is that it illustrates where utterances that spaCy will process can come from in a bot application. In the examples in previous chapters, we used utterances hardcoded in scripts. This is the first time you can see how real chatbots obtain their input.

Expanding the Chatbot

Now that you generally know how to integrate a chatbot that uses spaCy into Telegram, let's create a more interesting bot. For example, you might enhance the bot's functionality in the previous section so it extracts the intent from a user's message rather than just printing a message that the request is being processed. To accomplish this, you could recycle a script from one of the previous chapters.

Go back to the script in "Recognizing Synonyms Using Predefined Lists" on page 117 in Chapter 8, which uses lists of synonyms to extract the intent from a submitted utterance. Put the code from this script into a separate function, say, extract_intent(), which should take a single parameter—the text of a user's message as a Doc object (be sure to exclude the line of code with the hardcoded utterance at the beginning of the script as well as the line that prints the intent at the end). Additionally, the function you're creating must return a recognized intent as a string. In the script you're creating, place the new function above the callback function and revise the callback so it looks as follows:

```
...
def extract_intent(doc):
  #Put the code from Chapter 8 here

def utterance(update, context):
  msg = update.message.text
  nlp = spacy.load('en')
  doc = nlp(msg)
  for token in doc:
    if token.dep_ == 'dobj':
    ❶ intent = extract_intent(doc)
    ❷ if intent == 'orderPizza':
        update.message.reply_text('We need some more information to place your
        order.')
      elif intent == 'showPizza':
```

```
      update.message.reply_text('Would you like to look at our menu?')
    else:
      update.message.reply_text('Your intent is not recognized.')
    return
  update.message.reply_text('Please rephrase your request. Be as specific as
  possible!')
...
```

We call the newly created extract_intent() function from within the
utterance callback to obtain the user's intent ❶. Then we take an appropriate action, depending on the intent obtained. In this example, we simply
send the user a relevant message ❷.

Although we could put the code from Chapter 8 into the callback function directly, doing so would decrease the overall readability of the code, so
it's considered bad practice.

Holding the State of the Current Chat

The bot you have now does more than simply evaluate a user's message;
it can recognize a user's intent. Still, this isn't enough to take orders from
users. The primary flaw is that the chatbot will use the same utterance callback function for each user input, even when the intent has been recognized
and it's time to ask the user additional questions.

To address this problem, you need to *hold the state* of the current chat so
your bot knows what questions have already been answered and what it still
has to ask. Then you'll need to modify the callback so it can process user
messages according to the chat's current state.

This bot could work as follows: if the chatbot hasn't yet discovered an
intent, it should ask the user to express it. After finding the intent, the bot
should switch to another question that is relevant to the conversation's current state.

To help you simplify this kind of implementation, the python-telegram-bot
library includes the ConversationHandler object; it allows you to define entry
points and states of the conversation by tying them to a handler.

An entry point—for example, a Telegram command like /start—is
attached to a handler that can trigger the start of a chat. The handler's callback must return the initial state of conversation; this action determines what
handler to use for the user message that follows. To change the state of conversation, the handler's callback returns a new state after replying to the user.

The following code includes fragments of a script that illustrates how
to change the conversation's state between a chatbot and a user using
ConversationHandler:

```
def start(update, context):
...
❶ return 'ORDERING'
def intent_ext(update, context):
...
❷ if context.user_data.has_key('intent'):
    return 'ADD_INFO'
```

```
        else:
            update.message.reply_text('Please rephrase your request.')
            return 'ORDERING'
def add_info(update, context):
...
    return ConversationHandler.END
def cancel(update, context):
...
    return ConversationHandler.END
...
def main():
...
    disp = updater.dispatcher
    conv_handler = ConversationHandler(
        entry_points=[CommandHandler('start', start)],
        states={
      ❶ 'ORDERING': [MessageHandler(Filters.text,
                                     intent_ext)
                     ],
            'ADD_INFO': [MessageHandler(Filters.text,
                                        add_info)
                        ],
        },
        fallbacks=[CommandHandler('cancel', cancel)]
    )
    disp.add_handler(conv_handler)
...
```

Using `ConversationHandler` lets us define several callback functions and
the order in which they should be called. A callback processes the user's
message, and depending on the processing results, might change the state
of the conversation flow.

In this example, the callback for the /start command switches the
conversation to the ORDERING state ❶, which means that the next message
coming in from the user will be processed by the intent_ext() function.
The reason is that the intent_ext() function is the callback that belongs to
the ORDERING state's handler ❸, as defined in the `ConversationHandler` object's
states dictionary.

Note that the chatbot can switch between states based on a conditional
logic, as illustrated in the intent_ext() function: there, the conversation's
state will change to ADD_INFO (the state in which you collect additional information) only if the intent has been recognized ❷.

Putting All the Pieces Together

Now that you have a cursory understanding of how to structure a Telegram
bot that follows a predefined conversation flow, let's look at what a full
implementation of such a script might look like. This bot needs to ask the
user a series of questions, one after another, to complete an order form.
Because this is a simplified example, the chatbot can process only one
intent, orderPizza, and ask a user to specify only the type of pizza when com-
pleting the order form.

The following script is broken into chunks representing each function definition:

```
import logging
import sys
import spacy
from telegram.ext import Updater, CommandHandler, MessageHandler, Filters, ConversationHandler
#allows you to obtain generic debug info
logger = logging.getLogger(__name__)
logging.basicConfig(stream=sys.stdout, level=logging.DEBUG)

def extract_intent(doc):
    #Here should be the code created as suggested in the Expanding the Chatbot section earlier
    ...
    return intent
```

The extract_intent() function extracts the intent from a submitted utterance. We'll call this function from within the intent_ext() callback function defined next. The code for extract_intent() isn't provided here, but you can use the code described earlier in "Expanding the Chatbot" on page 161.

```
def details_to_str(user_data):
    details = list()
    for key, value in user_data.items():
        details.append('{} - {}'.format(key, value))
    return "\n".join(details).join(['\n', '\n'])
```

The details_to_str() function simply converts the content of the user_data dictionary to a string. The user_data dictionary contains information that the chatbot will extract from the conversation, such as the kind of pizza and number of pizzas the user wants. The bot includes this information in the final message sent to the user.

So far, we have defined the helper functions that will be invoked—either directly or indirectly—from within the bot's callback functions. Let's now define the callback functions.

```
def start(update, context):
    update.message.reply_text('Hi! This is a pizza ordering app. Do you want to order something?')
    return 'ORDERING'
```

The start() function is the callback for the /start Telegram command. In other words, the chatbot calls this function upon starting a chat. The function returns the ORDERING state, which means that the next message received will be processed by the callback attached to the ORDERING state's handler (the intent_ext() function in this example).

```
def intent_ext(update, context):
    msg = update.message.text
    nlp = spacy.load('en')
    doc = nlp(msg)
    for token in doc:
```

```
    if token.dep_ == 'dobj':
      intent = extract_intent(doc)
      if intent == 'orderPizza':
        context.user_data['product'] = 'pizza'
        update.message.reply_text('We need some more information to place your order. What type
        of pizza do you want?')
        return 'ADD_INFO'
      else:
        update.message.reply_text('Your intent is not recognized. Please rephrase your request.')
        return 'ORDERING'
      return
  update.message.reply_text('Please rephrase your request. Be as specific as possible!')
```

For simplicity, the intent_ext() function used here can recognize only one intent: orderPizza. If it detects this intent, it returns the ADD_INFO state. Otherwise, it returns the ORDERING state, which will cause the intent_ext() function to be invoked again to process the next user message. The ADD_INFO state's handler can be implemented as follows:

```
def add_info(update, context):
  msg = update.message.text
  nlp = spacy.load('en')
  doc = nlp(msg)
  for token in doc:
    if token.dep_ == 'dobj':
      dobj = token
      for child in dobj.lefts:
        if child.dep_ == 'amod' or child.dep_ == 'compound':
          context.user_data['type'] = child.text
          user_data = context.user_data
          update.message.reply_text("Your order has been placed."
                                    "{}"
                                    "Have a nice day!".format(details_to_str(user_data)))
          return ConversationHandler.END
  update.message.reply_text("Cannot extract necessary info. Please try again.")
  return 'ADD_INFO'
```

The add_info() function is the callback for the ADD_INFO state handler. In this implementation, it expects that a user ordering pizza will specify the type of pizza they want, then switches the state to ConversationHandler.END, the last state, as follows:

```
def cancel(update, context):
    update.message.reply_text("Have a nice day!")
    return ConversationHandler.END
```

The cancel() function used here simply sends a goodbye message to the user and switches the state to ConversationHandler.END.

Finally, the main() function should look like this:

```
def main():
    #Replace TOKEN with a real token
```

```
updater = Updater("TOKEN", use_context=True)
disp = updater.dispatcher
conv_handler = ConversationHandler(
    entry_points=[CommandHandler('start', start)],
    states={
        'ORDERING': [MessageHandler(Filters.text,
                                    intent_ext)
                    ],
        'ADD_INFO': [MessageHandler(Filters.text,
                                    add_info)
                    ],
    },
    fallbacks=[CommandHandler('cancel', cancel)]
)
disp.add_handler(conv_handler)
updater.start_polling()
updater.idle()
if __name__ == '__main__':
    main()
```

As usual, a bot script's `main()` function orchestrates the bot execution process.

You can test the script using either the Telegram web app on a computer or the Telegram app on a smartphone. Figure 11-3 shows a screenshot from the Telegram web app when it's running the script.

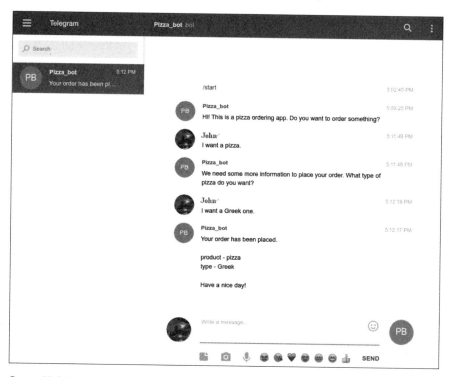

Figure 11-3: Testing your bot using the Telegram web app

Try This

Modify the script in the preceding section so it can recognize and process more intents than just `orderPizza`. Another relevant intent could be `showPizza`, meaning the user wants to look at the menu. To implement this, you'll need to modify the `intent_ext()` function, adding an `if intent == 'showPizza'` condition in the doc processing loop. Also, you'll need to add a new state to the `states` dictionary in the `ConversationHandler` object—say, `SHOW_MENU`—and implement the callback for it.

Summary

In this chapter, you learned how to implement and deploy a simple chatbot app using the Telegram bot platform, a popular messenger app. You learned how to define and hold states in a conversation. Notably, you also saw an example of where the user messages that you'd process with spaCy might actually come from.

12

IMPLEMENTING WEB DATA AND PROCESSING IMAGES

Real-life chatbots should respond to a variety of inputs, such as questions from users on unfamiliar topics or even images sent through messaging apps. For example, chatbot app users can send not only text messages, but also photos, and the bot is supposed to react appropriately to both.

This chapter provides some examples of how to use other libraries from Python's AI ecosystem when developing a bot application. First, you'll combine spaCy with Wikipedia to find information about keywords taken from a user's question. Next, you'll obtain descriptive tags for a submitted image with the help of Clarifai, an image and video recognition tool, so your app can interpret visual content.

Then you'll put all the components together to build a Telegram bot that can generate relevant responses to text and images by extracting information from Wikipedia.

How It Works

Figure 12-1 shows a diagram of the bot we'll build in this chapter. The bot is designed to understand text messages and pictures, and respond with text from Wikipedia.

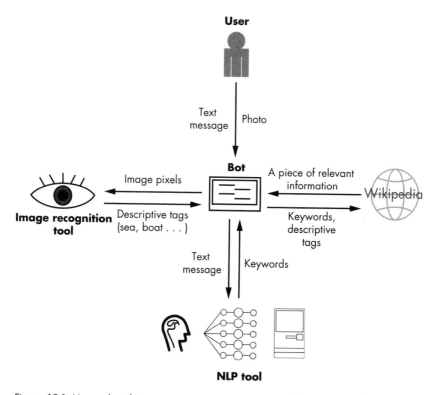

Figure 12-1: How a bot that can process text messages and pictures works

Using this bot, the user can post either a text message or a picture. If the post is a picture, the bot sends it to an image recognition tool for processing. This tool returns a verbal description of the picture in the form of descriptive tags. If the post is a text message, the bot uses an NLP tool like spaCy to extract a keyword or a keyphrase from it. The bot then uses either the tag or the keyphrase to find the most relevant content on Wikipedia (or somewhere else on the web) and return a piece of it to the user. You can use this scenario in chatbots you design to hold a conversation on various topics for fun, learning, or personal use.

Making Your Bot Find Answers to Questions from Wikipedia

Let's start with a discussion of techniques that you can implement in your bot to make it interpret a wide range of text messages. Previous chapters talked about how bots used for business purposes typically ask for certain information from the user and then use the answer to fill an order or booking request. In contrast, a bot designed to hold informal conversations should be able to answer a diverse range of user questions.

One way to help a chatbot answer user questions is to choose a keyword or keyphrase in the question that provides a clue as to what information should be included in the answer. Once you have this keyword or keyphrase, you can use it to search for the answer using tools like the Wikipedia API for Python. Wikipedia's API lets you access and parse Wikipedia content programmatically, performing a search for a keyword to retrieve content from the most relevant Wikipedia article. The following sections describe how to do this.

But before proceeding to the examples, make sure you're using one of the most recent spaCy models, because the accuracy of the dependency parsing is higher in newer versions. You can check the version of your current model using the following command:

```
nlp.meta['version']
```

Then visit the *https://explosion.ai/demos/display/* demo page (discussed in Chapter 7) to see the latest stable versions of spaCy models available. Alternatively, you can visit spaCy's documentation at *https://spacy.io/usage/* to check for the newest version of spaCy. Both spaCy and its models follow the same versioning scheme. Based on that information, you might want to update the model you currently use. Refer to Chapter 2 for details on how to download and install a spaCy model.

Determining What the Question Is About

Some words in a question are more important than others when you're trying to determine what the speaker is asking about. Sometimes it's enough to look at a single word in the question, such as the noun that follows a preposition. For example, a user might use any of the following questions to ask the bot to find some information about rhinos:

```
Have you heard of rhinos? Are you familiar with rhinos? What could you tell me about rhinos?
```

Let's look at what the dependency parsing of such sentences might look like. Figure 12-2 shows a graphical representation of the parsing of the first sentence.

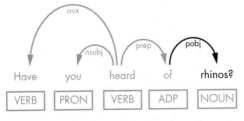

Figure 12-2: The dependency parsing of a sentence containing an object of a preposition

The parsing illustrates that in this kind of question you can get the word "rhinos" by extracting the object of the preposition. "Rhinos" would be the most helpful word in the question for finding an answer. The following code fragment shows how you might extract the first occurrence of an object of the preposition in the question:

```
doc = nlp(u"Have you heard of rhinos?")
for t in doc:
  if t.dep_ == 'pobj' and (t.pos_ == 'NOUN' or t.pos_ == 'PROPN'):
    phrase = (' '.join([child.text for child in t.lefts]) + ' ' + t.text).lstrip()
    break
```

In the code, we also pick up the left children of the object of the preposition, because the object might have important modifiers, as in the following example: "What can you say about wild mountain goats?" When given this question, the code should assign "wild mountain goats" to the phrase variable.

Notice the use of the break statement at the end, which guarantees that only the first object of a preposition in a sentence will be picked up. For example, in the sentence, "Tell me about the United States of America," the phrase "the United States" would be picked up, but not "America."

But this is not always desirable behavior. What if a user asked, "Tell me about the color of the sky."? This is where we need to apply more complicated logic. In particular, we might want to to pick up any prepositional object that follows the first prepositional object, provided the latter is dependent on the former.

Here is how you might implement this logic:

```
doc = nlp(u"Tell me about the color of the sky.")
for t in doc:
  if t.dep_ == 'pobj' and (t.pos_ == 'NOUN' or t.pos_ == 'PROPN'):
    phrase = (' '.join([child.text for child in t.lefts]) + ' ' + t.text).lstrip()
    if bool([prep for prep in t.rights if prep.dep_ == 'prep']):
      prep = list(t.rights)[0]
      pobj = list(prep.children)[0]
      phrase = phrase + ' ' + prep.text + ' ' + pobj.text
    break
```

Note that this code will process a prepositional object that is a dependent of the first prepositional object only if the former exists in the sentence. Otherwise, this code will work the same as the code shown previously.

Now let's look at another type of question in the following examples where two words, a verb and its subject, provide the best information about what a user wants in response to the questions:

```
Do you know what an elephant eats? Tell me how dolphins sleep. What is an API?
```

Figure 12-3 shows what a dependency parsing for one of these sentences might look like.

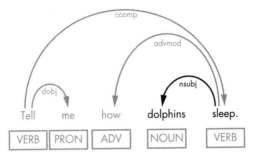

Figure 12-3: The dependency parsing of a sentence in which a subject/verb pair is the most informative element for discovering what the speaker wants to know

Looking through the parsing shown in the figure, notice that the subject/verb pair that occurs at the end of the sentence is the most informative when trying to determine what the speaker asks about. Programmatically, you can extract the subject and verb pair from a sentence using the following code:

```
doc = nlp(u"Do you know what an elephant eats?")
for t in reversed(doc):
  if t.dep_ == 'nsubj' and (t.pos_ == 'NOUN' or t.pos_ == 'PROPN'):
    phrase = t.text + ' ' + t.head.text
    break
```

While examining this code, notice that we loop backward from the end of the sentence using Python's reversed() function. The reason is that we need to pick up the last subject/verb pair in the sentence, as in this example: "Do you know what an elephant eats?" In this sentence, we're interested in the phrase "elephant eats" rather than "you know," which is also a subject/verb pair.

Additionally, in some questions, the last noun in the sentence is the direct object of a verb that matters to determine what the question is about, as in the following example:

```
How to feed a cat?
```

In this sentence, extracting the direct object "cat" wouldn't be sufficient, because we also need the word "feed" to understand the question. Ideally, we'd generate the keyphrase "feeding a cat." That is, we'd replace the infinitive "to" form of the verb with a gerund by adding "-ing," optimizing the keyphrase for an internet search. Figure 12-4 shows the dependency parsing for this sentence.

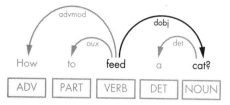

Figure 12-4: Dependency parsing of a sentence with a
verb/direct object pair as the most informative phrase

This syntactic parsing shows that extracting the required phrase is
easy, because the direct object and its transitive verb are connected with a
direct link.

The code implementation for the extraction discussed here might look
like this:

```
doc = nlp(u"How to feed a cat?")
for t in reversed(doc):
  if t.dep_ == 'dobj' and (t.pos_ == 'NOUN' or t.pos_ == 'PROPN'):
    phrase = t.head.lemma_ + 'ing' + ' ' + t.text
    break
```

In this case, we once again loop backward from the end of the sentence. To understand why, consider the following sentence: "Tell me something about how to feed a cat." It contains two verb/direct object pairs, but
we're interested only in the one that occurs at the end of the sentence.

Try This

Modify the code in the previous section that extracts the phrase "elephant
eats" so the keyphrase being extracted from the sentence includes possible
modifiers of the subject, excluding a possible determiner. For example,
in the sentence, "Tell me how a female cheetah hunts," your script should
return "female cheetah hunts" and remove the "a" determiner from the
noun chunk. As an example of how you might implement this, look at the
code that follows Figure 12-2. In that code, you picked up modifiers for the
object of the preposition being extracted.

Also, add a check to see whether the verb included in the phrase being
extracted has a direct object, and if so, append the direct object to the keyphrase. For example, the question "Do you know how many eggs a sea turtle
lays?" should give you the following keyphrase: "sea turtle lays eggs."

Using Wikipedia to Answer User Questions

Now that you have a keyphrase that can help you find the information
needed to generate a relevant response to the user's question, you need to
retrieve the information. A bot can get answers to user questions from several places, and the proper source to use depends on the application, but

Wikipedia is a good place to start. The `wikipedia` Python library (*https://pypi .org/project/wikipedia/*) allows you to access Wikipedia articles from within your Python code.

You can install the library via `pip` as follows:

```
pip install wikipedia
```

To test the newly installed library, use the following script, which relies on a code fragment from the previous section to extract a keyword from a submitted sentence. Then it uses that keyword as a Wikipedia search term.

```
import spacy
import wikipedia
nlp = spacy.load('en')
doc = nlp(u"What do you know about rhinos?")
for t in doc:
    if t.dep_ == 'pobj' and (t.pos_ == 'NOUN' or t.pos_ == 'PROPN'):
    ❶ phrase = (' '.join([child.text for child in t.lefts]) + ' ' + t.text).
      lstrip()
      break
❷ wiki_resp = wikipedia.page(phrase)
print("Article title: ", wiki_resp.title)
print("Article url: ", wiki_resp.url)
print("Article summary: ", wikipedia.summary(phrase, sentences=1))
```

In this script, we extract a keyword or keyphrase from the submitted sentence ❶ and send it to the `wikipedia.page()` function, which returns the most relevant article for the given keyword ❷. Then we simply print out the article's title, URL, and first sentence.

The output this script generates should look like this:

```
Article title:  Rhinoceros
Article url:  https://en.wikipedia.org/wiki/Rhinoceros
Article summary:  A rhinoceros (, from Greek  rhinokerōs, meaning 'nose-horned', from  rhis,
meaning 'nose', and  keras, meaning 'horn'), commonly abbreviated to rhino, is one of ...
```

Try This

Enhance the script in the previous section so it can "see" the children of the first prepositional object and the dependent prepositional objects. For example, in the question, "Have you heard of fried eggs with yellow tomatoes?" it should extract the keyphrase "fried eggs with yellow tomatoes."

Reacting to Images Sent in a Chat

In addition to text messages, users of messenger apps often post images. Other people usually respond to these with comments about what is shown in the picture. For example, a user posts a photo of grapes, to which another user leaves the following comment: "I love fruit. It contains lots of fiber and vitamins." How can you teach a bot to do the same? One way is to generate descriptive tags for an image that the bot can use in processing. This is where you need an image recognition tool, like Clarifai, which provides built-in models trained with photos from different domains, such as apparel, travel, or celebrities.

Clarifai allows a bot to obtain a set of categories for a submitted photo, making it possible for the bot to guess what is depicted in the image. You can get useful categories for a photo in two steps. First, you use Clarifai's general image recognition model to obtain descriptive tags (objects with probabilities) that can give you a general idea of what is shown in the photo. For example, the presence of the "no person" tag indicates that no people are in the photo.

Second, after examining the tags, you can apply more specific models to the same photo, such as Clarifai's Food or Apparel models. Both are trained to recognize food and fashion-related items, respectively. This time, you'll obtain another, more granular set of tags to give you a better idea of the contents of the photo. For the entire list of Clarifai's image recognition models, visit its Models page at *https://www.clarifai.com/models/*.

Generating Descriptive Tags for Images Using Clarifai

Clarifai offers a Python client to interact with its recognition API. You can install the latest stable package using pip:

```
pip install clarifai --upgrade
```

Before you can start using the Clarifai library, you must obtain an API key by creating an account and then clicking the **GET API KEY** button at *https://www.clarifai.com/*.

Once you have the key, you can test the Clarifai library. The following simple script passes an image to a Clarifai model and prints a list of tags expressing possible categories for the image:

```
from clarifai.rest import ClarifaiApp, client, Image
app = ClarifaiApp(api_key='YOUR_API_KEY')
❶ model = app.public_models.general_model
filename = '/your_path/grape.jpg'
❷ image = Image(file_obj=open(filename, 'rb'))
response = model.predict([image])
❸ concepts = response['outputs'][0]['data']['concepts']
for concept in concepts:
    print(concept['name'], concept['value'])
```

In this example, we call Clarifai's Predict API with the general model ❶. Clarifai takes only the pixels as input, so make sure you're opening an image file in 'rb' mode ❷, which opens the file in binary format for reading. The

Predict API generates a list of descriptive tags, such as fruit, grape, health, and so on ❸, for the submitted photo, allowing the code to "understand" what it shows.

The *grape.jpg* file used in this example contains the photo shown in Figure 12-5.

Figure 12-5: The photo submitted to Clarifai in the preceding script

The list of concepts that the script generates for the photo should look as follows:

```
no person 0.9968359470367432
wine 0.9812138080596924
fruit 0.9805494546890259
juicy 0.9788177013397217
health 0.9755384922027588
grow 0.9669009447097778
grape 0.9660607576370239
...
```

Each entry represents a category and the probability that the image fits within the category. Thus, the first tag in the list tells us that the submitted photo contains no person with a probability of 0.99. Note that not all the tags will provide a direct description of the depicted content. For example, the tag "wine" is included here, perhaps because wine is made from grapes. The presence of indirect tags in the list gives your bot more options to interpret the image.

Using Tags to Generate Text Responses to Images

Now that you know how to obtain descriptive tags for an image, how can you use these tags to respond to the image? Or how can you choose the most important tags from the generated list? Think about the following general considerations:

- You might want to take into account only the tags with high likelihoods. For that, you can choose a threshold of likelihood for the tags. For example, consider only the top five or 10 tags.
- You might choose only those tags that are in the context of the current chat. Chapter 11 showed an example of how to maintain the context of the current chat in a Telegram bot using the `context.user_data` dictionary.
- You might iterate over the generated tags, searching for a particular tag. For example, you might search for the tag "fruit" or "health" to determine whether you should continue the conversation on this topic.

The bot discussed in the next section will implement the third option.

Putting All the Pieces Together in a Telegram Bot

In the rest of this chapter, we'll build a Telegram chatbot that uses the Wikipedia API and the Clarifai API. This bot will respond intelligently to text and images of food. Refer back to Chapter 11 for details on how to create a new bot in Telegram.

Importing the Libraries

The import section of the code must include all the libraries that we'll use in the bot's code. In this example, we include the libraries required to access the Telegram Bot API, Wikipedia API, Clarifai API, and spaCy.

```
import spacy
import wikipedia
from telegram.ext import Updater, CommandHandler, MessageHandler, Filters
from clarifai.rest import ClarifaiApp, Image
```

If you've followed the instructions provided in this chapter and Chapter 11, all of these libraries should be available on your system.

Writing the Helper Functions

Next, we need to implement the helper functions that will be invoked from within the bot's callback functions. The `keyphrase()` function takes a sentence as a Doc object and tries to extract the most informative word or a phrase from it, as discussed earlier in "Determining What the Question Is About" on page 171. The following implementation uses the code fragments you saw in that section, adjusting them so we can use them within a single function:

```
def keyphrase(doc):
  for t in doc:
    if t.dep_ == 'pobj' and (t.pos_ == 'NOUN' or t.pos_ == 'PROPN'):
      return (' '.join([child.text for child in t.lefts]) + ' ' + t.text).
      lstrip()
  for t in reversed(doc):
    if t.dep_ == 'nsubj' and (t.pos_ == 'NOUN' or t.pos_ == 'PROPN'):
      return t.text + ' ' + t.head.text
  for t in reversed(doc):
    if t.dep_ == 'dobj' and (t.pos_ == 'NOUN' or t.pos_ == 'PROPN'):
      return t.head.text + 'ing' + ' ' + t.text
  return False
```

Note that the conditions are arranged in order of priority in this code. Thus, if the object of the preposition is found, we extract it and quit without checking for the other conditions. Of course, some complicated questions might meet multiple conditions, but checking for this would complicate the function implementation.

Like the keyphrase() function, the photo_tags() function is supposed to determine the most descriptive word for a user's input. But unlike keyphrase(), it analyzes a photo. It performs the analysis with the help of Clarifai, which generates a set of descriptive tags for a submitted photo. This implementation uses only two Clarifai models: the general model and the food model.

```
def photo_tags(filename):
  app = ClarifaiApp(api_key=CLARIFAI_API_KEY)
  model = app.public_models.general_model
  image = Image(file_obj=open(filename, 'rb'))
  response = model.predict([image])
  concepts = response['outputs'][0]['data']['concepts']
  for concept in concepts:
    if concept['name'] == 'food':
      food_model = app.public_models.food_model
      result = food_model.predict([image])
      first_concept = result['outputs'][0]['data']['concepts'][0]['name']
      return first_concept
  return response['outputs'][0]['data']['concepts'][1]['name']
```

This code starts by applying the general model. If the tag 'food' is found in the generated list, it applies the food model to obtain more descriptive tags for the food items shown in the image. This implementation will use the first tag only as the keyword for the search.

Now that we have the keyword or keyphrase, determined either in the keyphrase() function or in the photo_tags() function, we need to obtain a piece of information that is closely related to this keyword or keyphrase. The following wiki() function does the trick:

```
def wiki(concept):
  nlp = spacy.load('en')
  wiki_resp = wikipedia.page(concept)
  doc = nlp(wiki_resp.content)
  if len(concept.split()) == 1:
    for sent in doc.sents:
      for t in sent:
        if t.text == concept and t.dep_ == 'dobj':
          return sent.text
  return list(doc.sents)[0].text
```

The algorithm we use here searches for a sentence in the retrieved content that includes the keyword as the direct object.

But this simple implementation can intelligently process only a single-word input. When a word is submitted, the algorithm we use here just extracts the first sentence from the Wikipedia article found with the help of this word.

Writing the Callback and main() Functions

Next, we add the bot's callback functions. The start() function simply sends a greeting to the user in response to the /start command.

```
def start(update, context):
    update.message.reply_text('Hi! This is a conversational bot. Ask me something.')
```

The text_msg() function is the callback for the bot's user text messages handler.

```
def text_msg(update, context):
  msg = update.message.text
  nlp = spacy.load('en')
  doc = nlp(msg)
  concept = keyphrase(doc)
  if concept != False:
    update.message.reply_text(wiki(concept))
  else:
    update.message.reply_text('Please rephrase your question.')
```

First, we apply spaCy's pipeline to the message, converting it to a Doc object. Then we send the Doc to the keyphrase() function discussed earlier to extract a keyword or keyphrase from the message. The returned keyword or keyphrase is then sent to the wiki() function to obtain a piece of relevant information, which should be a single sentence in this implementation.

The photo() function shown in the following code is the callback for the bot's handler for the photos submitted by the user:

```
def photo(update, context):
    photo_file = update.message.photo[-1].get_file()
    filename = '{}.jpg'.format(photo_file.file_id)
    photo_file.download(filename)
    concept = photo_tags(filename)
    update.message.reply_text(wiki(concept))
```

The function retrieves the submitted image as a file and sends it for further processing to the helper functions discussed earlier in "Writing the Helper Functions" on page 178.

Finally, we add the main() function in which we register handlers for both text messages and photos.

```
def main():
    updater = Updater("YOUR_TOKEN", use_context=True)
    disp = updater.dispatcher
    disp.add_handler(CommandHandler("start", start))
    disp.add_handler(MessageHandler(Filters.text, text_msg))
    disp.add_handler(MessageHandler(Filters.photo, photo))
    updater.start_polling()
    updater.idle()
if __name__ == '__main__':
    main()
```

The main() function for this Telegram bot is quite concise. We create the Updater and pass the bot's token to it. Then we obtain the dispatcher to register handlers. In this example, we register just three handlers. The first one is the handler for the /start command. The second handles text messages coming from the user. The third one handles photos posted by the user. After registering handlers, we start the bot by invoking updater.start _polling() and then invoking updater.idle() to block the script to wait for a user message or an exit shortcut (CTRL-C).

Testing the Bot

Now that we've created the bot, it's time to test it. You can test it either on a smartphone or a computer. On a smartphone, in the Telegram app search for your bot's name followed by the @ sign, and then enter the /start command to start a chat. On a computer, use Telegram Web at *https://web.telegram.org*.

After receiving a greeting from the bot, send it a simple request, such as "Tell me about fruit." The bot should respond with a single sentence that it extracts from a relevant Wikipedia article. For simplicity, choose a sentence that uses the direct object from the sentence ("fruit" in this example) as the keyword.

You can also submit a photo to check which comment the bot will give in response. Figure 12-6 illustrates a screenshot of such a test.

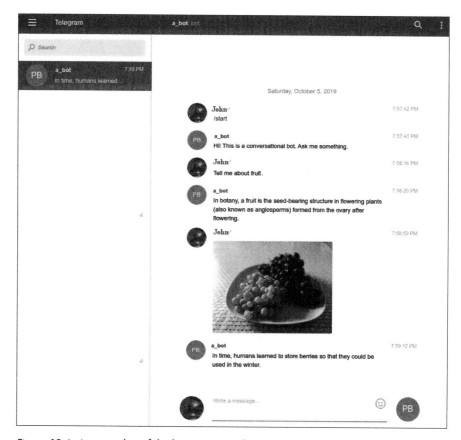

Figure 12-6: A screenshot of the bot we created

Remember that this implementation can properly process only photos of food.

Try This

Note that the bot implementation provided in the preceding section can't generate smart responses to many different types of user input. The `wiki()` function we used can properly process only those requests for which `keyphrase()` returns a single word. It also works best if that keyword is a direct object. Also, the bot can only intelligently respond to images of food.

Enhance the `wiki()` function so it can process phrases instead of only one word, such as "dolphins sleep." Finding an appropriate sentence for such a phrase requires using dependency labels, because you'll need to find a subject/verb pair. In addition, you'll need to reduce the words to their lemmas. For example, "dolphins sleep" and "dolphin sleeps" should satisfy the search criteria.

You might also want to enhance the functionality of the `photo_tags()` function so it can process not only food photos, but also those that show something else—for example, apparel.

Summary

In this chapter, you saw examples of how to use spaCy along with other libraries in Python's AI ecosystem to build an AI-powered application that can process data of different types. By using the Wikipedia and Clarifai Python APIs, we designed a chatbot that could react to images and pull text from Wikipedia, techniques that make the bot a smarter interlocutor.

After reading this book, you might want to expand and improve on what you've learned. The most natural way to enhance your knowledge is to continue to experiment with chatbots. Start by building a Telegram script with Python using the instructions provided in Chapter 11; next, enhance its functionality using instructions provided in this chapter. Then work on improving the algorithms you learned in this book to make them more suitable for your use cases.

LINGUISTIC PRIMER

Most of the chapters in the book focus on analyzing sentence structures to identify patterns in word sequences using spaCy.

To understand sentence analysis and patterns, you need some basic knowledge of linguistics. This appendix contains a linguistic primer to use as a reference.

Dependency Grammars vs. Phrase Structure Grammars

By default, spaCy uses a dependency grammar rather than a phrase structure grammar more commonly used in linguistics. This section explains the difference between these two grammar types. If you have a formal linguistic background, you may find this information helpful.

Also known as a constituent-based grammar, a *phrase structure grammar* models natural language based on how words combine to form constituents in a sentence. In syntax, a *constituent* is a group of words that functions as a single unit in a sentence. The phrase structure rules decompose a sentence into its constituent parts, forming a tree structure that begins with individual words and builds up larger and larger constituents.

In contrast, a *dependency grammar* is a word-based grammar that focuses on the relations between individual words rather than between constituents. As a result, a dependency parse, like the ones shown throughout this book, forms a tree that reflects how words relate to other words in a sentence.

Figure A-1 shows an example of a sentence parsing using both grammar types.

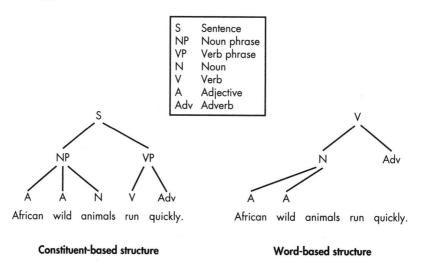

Constituent-based structure   Word-based structure

Figure A-1: An example of tree structures for a constituent-based phrase structure grammar (left) and a word-based dependency grammar (right)

The phrase structure tree breaks up the sentence based on the fact that the sentence consists of a noun phrase and a verb phrase. Those phrases appear on the second level of the hierarchy, directly under the sentence (S) mark—the formal top level. On the bottom level are the individual words that make up those phrases.

In contrast, the dependency structure uses the verb as the structural center of a sentence. The other words are either directly or indirectly connected to this verb with the help of directed links, known as *dependencies*. The dependency grammar that spaCy uses by default expresses the grammatical structure of a sentence as a set of one-to-one correspondences between words.

Each of these relations represents a grammatical function in which one word is the *child*, or the dependent word, and the other is the *head*, or the governor. For example, in the pair "blue sky," the dominant word is "sky," and "blue"—its modifier—is its subordinate. You can think of the head as the word with the most relative "importance" and without which the child doesn't make sense. By contrast, the head of a relation can often stand in a sentence without the child (for example, you don't need "African" or "wild" in the sentence shown in Figure A-1, nor "quickly").

Figure A-2 shows a graphical depiction of this concept.

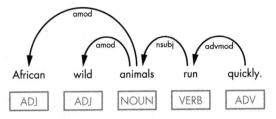

Figure A-2: An example of a dependency tree structure based on the head/child concept

Notice that the dependency tree shown in Figure A-2 is similar to the representation on the right in Figure A-1. The only difference between these two representations is a visual one: although the tree shown in Figure A-1 has a pyramidal view, the tree in Figure A-2 uses labeled, directed arcs to emphasize the head/child link.

Each word in a sentence must be connected to exactly one head. But the same word might have none, one, or several children. The spaCy grammar assumes that the head of a sentence (the ROOT token) is its own head. In this example, the verb "run" is the head of the sentence, so the head property of the Token object representing this word will refer to this same Token object.

Note that the head/child relationship has nothing to do with linear order in the sentence. For example, the child "wild" comes before its head "animals," but the child "quickly" comes after its head "run."

Common Grammar Concepts

This section discusses the more advanced grammar concepts used in the book, including transitive verbs and direct objects, prepositional objects, modal auxiliary verbs, and personal pronouns.

Transitive Verbs and Direct Objects

A *direct object* is a noun (or a noun phrase) denoting something that is directly acted on by a verb. A *transitive verb* accepts a direct object. In most cases, for identifying intent, the transitive verb and its direct object are the most important words in a sentence to extract. The reason is that these words typically best describe the action and the thing acted upon. For example, in the sentence, "I want a pizza," the words "want" and "pizza" express the sentence's intent.

Prepositional Objects

A *preposition* connects noun phrases with other words in a sentence. Prepositions such as "in," "above," "under," "after," and "before" express spatial or temporal relations. Others, such as "to," "of," and "for," indicate semantic roles. For instance, in the sentence, "You'll find the envelope under the book," the preposition "under" expresses a spatial relationship between the envelope and the book. And in the sentence, "I will deploy it to a channel," the use of the preposition "to" indicates the role goal expressed by the prepositional phrase "a channel."

An *object of a preposition* (known as a complement in theoretical linguistics) is a noun, pronoun, or noun phrase that follows a preposition. In the sentence, "I wrote a series of articles," the word "articles" is the object of the preposition.

In some questions, extracting the object of the preposition might give you the most informative word or phrase in terms of finding the answer, as shown in the question, "What can be done about climate change?" The phrase "climate change" is the key phrase in determining what the question is about.

The spaCy dependency parser indexes prepositions as `'prep'` and objects of the preposition as `'pobj'`.

Modal Auxiliary Verbs

Modal auxiliary verbs include "may," "might," "can," "could," "must," "ought," "shall," "should," "will," and "would," among others. They're used in conjunction with a main verb in the base form to indicate *modality*—in other words, likelihood, permission, capability, necessity, willingness, or advice.

The spaCy part-of-speech tagger recognizes modal auxiliary verbs, marking them with the fine-grained part-of-speech tag `'MD'`. The syntactic dependency parser marks them as `'aux'`. You might need to check whether a sentence uses a modal auxiliary verb when you need, for example, to reconstruct the sentence from a question.

Personal Pronouns

A personal pronoun refers to a specific person, object, or to multiple people or objects. In English, personal pronouns have a number of forms, distinguished according to their grammatical role in a sentence:

- The nominative form (I, you, he, she, it, we, they) is typically used as the nominal subject of a verb.
- The accusative form (me, you, him, her, it, us, them) is typically used as the object of a verb or preposition.
- The reflexive form (myself, yourself/yourselves, himself, herself, itself, ourselves, themselves) typically refers back to the subject specified within the same clause.

The spaCy parser assigns different dependency labels to personal pronouns according to their forms. Thus, a personal pronoun in nominative form is usually assigned the `'nsubj'` dependency label, which stands for "nominal subject." It is interesting to note that in many user-generated sentences for chatbots, the subject of the sentence is "I."

In accusative form, a personal pronoun can be assigned either `'dobj'` or `'iobj'`, which stands for direct object and indirect object, respectively. Reflexive pronouns also usually act as either direct objects or indirect objects.

INDEX

dependency parsing
    convolutional neural networks
        (CNNs) and, 11
    customizing, 149–153
    syntactic dependency parsing, 3, 24
    visualizing, 100–101
dependency tree structures, 5, 86–91
dependent words, 186
descriptive tags, 176–178
det label, 26
determine_question_type function, 60
dimensions, 65–66
direct objects, 112–117, 187
discourse, 122–125
displaCy dependency visualizer, 98–99
displaCy named entity visualizer, 99–100
displaCy web servers, 100–101
displacy.render() method, 106–107
displacy.serve() method, 106–107
DISTRICT label, 40
dobj label, 25–26
Doc objects, 18, 32
doc.noun_chunks containers, 35
doc.sents containers, 33–35

E

echo() function, 159
EntityRecognizer class, 40
'ents' option, 104–106
errors
    missing INTO keyword, 7
    training process and, 142
Explosion AI website, 97
extract_intent() function, 161, 164

F

Facebook Messenger, 157
fastText, 65
financial data, 49–50
fine-grained parts of speech tags,
    22, 49
for loops, 34, 53–54, 59
from_disk() method, 42

G

generate_question function, 60
Gensim, xvi

get_utterance function, 86
governors, 186

H

handlers, 156
head/child syntactic relations, 25, 87,
    186–187
helper functions, 178–180
hex color codes, 106

I

idle() method, 160
images, 175–178
inflections, 6
information questions, 56–57
INSERT statements, 137, 138
intent identifiers, 112
interchange formats, 129–130
    JSON, 129–133
    XML, 129
inversion, 52

J

JJ tag, 22
JSON, 129–133

K

keyphrase() function, 178–180
keywords, 12, 67–68, 86–91

L

leftward syntactic dependencies, 33
lemmas, 18–21
linguistics, 185–188
loanwords, 6
loss, 142

M

machine learning, xvii, 3–8
main() function, 165–166
Matcher, 79–80
meaning transition, 13
meanings, 65–66
messaging apps, 157

minibatch() method, 147
missing INTO keyword error, 7
modal auxiliary verbs, 188
model training, 4
modifiers, 94–95
money, 49–50
multiple intents, 113–114
MySQL databases, 135–138

N

named entities, 29, 72–74
named entity recognition, 4, 29,
    143–144
natural language processing (NLP),
    xv–xvi, 1–2
Natural Language Toolkit (NLTK), xvi
ner component, 42
ner.add_label() method, 41
neural networks, 9–11
nlp.begin_training() method, 147
nlp.meta attribute, 39
NN tag, 22
NNS tag, 22
nominative form, 188
noun chunks, 33–35
nsubj label, 26
numbers, 133–135
numeric tags, 48–49

O

objects of a preposition, 188
objects vs. subjects, 55–56
optimizers, 147
options argument, 103–106
ORG label, 40
Oxford English Dictionary, 6

P

part-of-speech tags, 3–4, 21–24, 48–54
    JJ, 22
    NN, 22
    NNS, 22
    PRP, 22, 51–54
    PRP$, 22, 51
    VB, 22, 23
    VBD, 22

    VBG, 22, 23
    VBZ, 56
patterns, 76–86
personal pronouns, 52, 188
photo_tags() function, 179–180
photo() function, 181
phrase structure grammars, 185–187
pipelines, 17–18, 37–42, 146
pobj label, 26–28
pos_pattern function, 81, 83–85
possessive pronouns, 52
postmodifiers, 94
predefined lists, 117–119
premodifiers, 94
prepositional objects, 187–188
preprocessing, 71–72, 128
present tense progressive aspect, 22
probability distributions, 8
processing pipelines, 17–18, 37–42
proforms, 122–125
pron_pattern function, 82–85
pronouns, 51–54, 82–83, 188
    personal, 52, 188
    possessive, 52
    reflexive, 188
PRP tag, 22, 51–54
PRP$ tag, 22, 51
punctuation tags, 48–49
python-telegram-bot library, 158–159
.pyx files, 43

Q

question_type variable, 58–59
questions, 56–60, 171–175

R

reflexive pronouns, 188
relational databases, 127–139
rendering, 100
ROOT label, 26–28
row-and-column databases, 127–139

S

scientific terms, 6
semantic relations, 149–153
semantic similarity, 3, 120–121

sentence-by-sentence visualizations, 102–103
shredding the discourse, 28
similarity method, 63, 66–67
slang, 6
spaCy library, xvi–xvii
spacy.explain() function, 48, 143
spacy.load() function, 38
spacy.util.get_lang_class() function, 40
Span objects, 36
span.merge() function, 36
special cases, 21
split infinitives, 6
SQL, 131
start() function, 164, 180
start_polling() method, 160
statistical models, 8–11, 16–17
structured data, 128–132
subjects vs. objects, 55–56
substitutes, 123–124
symbolic tags, 48–49
synonyms, 3, 117–119
syntactic dependencies
    overview, 24–28
    keywords and, 86–91
    leftward, 33
    parsing, 3
    syntactic dependency labels, 24–26. *See also* dependency labels
    text processing, 55–60

T

Telegram, 157–166, 178–183
text content, 18
third-party word vectors, 68–69
to_disk() method, 42, 148
token.conjuncts, 113–114
tokens, 18, 32
training examples, 142–144
transitive verbs, 112–117, 187

U

unstructured data, 128–132
user's intent, 12
utterances, 77–79

V

VB tag, 22, 23
VBD tag, 22
VBG tag, 22, 23
VBZ tag, 56
vectors, 64–65
verbs
    auxiliary, 188
    modal auxiliary, 188
    transitive, 112–117, 187
visualizations
    customizing, 103–106
    dependency parsing, 100–101
    displaCy dependency visualizer, 98–99
    displaCy named entity visualizer, 99–100
    exporting, 106–107
    sentence-by-sentence, 102–103
vocab objects, 32

W

web color names, 106
while loops, 50
wiki() function, 180
Wikipedia, 170–175, 178–183
word embedding, 2–3
word lists, 115–117
word sequence patterns, 76–86
word vectors
    overview, 64–68
    calculating similarity using, 69–74
    installing, 68–69
    third-party word vectors, 68–69
word2int() function, 134
word2vec algorithm, xvi
word-based dependency grammars, 186
working environment set up, 16

X

XML, 129

Y

yes/no questions, 56–57

Natural Language Processing with Python and spaCy is set in New Baskerville, Futura, Dogma, and TheSansMono Condensed. The book was printed and bound by Sheridan Books, Inc. in Chelsea, Michigan. The paper is 60# Finch Offset, which is certified by the Forest Stewardship Council (FSC).

The book uses a layflat binding, in which the pages are bound together with a cold-set, flexible glue and the first and last pages of the resulting book block are attached to the cover. The cover is not actually glued to the book's spine, and when open, the book lies flat and the spine doesn't crack.

RESOURCES

Visit *https://nostarch.com/nlppython/* for errata and more information.

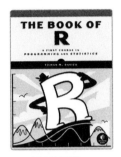

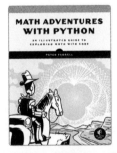

The Electronic Frontier Foundation (EFF) is the leading organization defending civil liberties in the digital world. We defend free speech on the Internet, fight illegal surveillance, promote the rights of innovators to develop new digital technologies, and work to ensure that the rights and freedoms we enjoy are enhanced — rather than eroded — as our use of technology grows.

EFF.ORG

ELECTRONIC FRONTIER FOUNDATION

Protecting Rights and Promoting Freedom on the Electronic Frontier